The

CONSTANTINE

DOCTRINE

CHRISTIAN LEADERSHIP IN WESTERN CIVILIZATION

JEFF DARVILLE

FREILING

PUBLISHING

Scriptures are taken from:

The Holy Bible, English Standard Version. ESV® Text Edition: 2016. Copyright © 2001 by Crossway Bibles, a publishing ministry of Good News Publishers.

The Holy Bible, New International Version®, NIV® Copyright © 1973, 1978, 1984, 2011 by Biblica, Inc.® Used by permission. All rights reserved worldwide.

Published by Freiling Publishing, a division of Freiling Agency, LLC.

P.O. Box 1264
Warrenton, VA 20188

www.FreilingPublishing.com

PB ISBN: 978-1-956267-48-8
e-Book ISBN: 978-1-956267-50-1

Printed in the United States of America

"I am not ashamed of the gospel,
because it is the power of God that brings salvation to everyone
who believes: first to the Jew, then to the Gentile."

Romans 1:16

Dedication

JESUS IS MY Lord and God, my rock, and my salvation. To whom shall I turn? You have the power of life and death in your hands.

Thank you to my parents, Wayne and Yvonne Darville, who raised God-fearing, Christ-loving, American Flag-waving children. My siblings, Josh, Kristin, and Kyle, all immeasurably impacted my life. Thank you for your love and support. Our family is strong, we enjoy life to the Glory of God, encourage and care deeply about one another, cry in one voice, and worship unified.

My wife, Elaine, you are the light of my life. I love you. Our lives fit together, we have spent so many wonderful days and years together. Elizabeth and Michael, I love you. I will always be proud of you, teach and train you in the way that you should go, and fight for you when needed.

Friends are a true gift from God. Rob, Matt, Jordan, and Doug, I could not ask for godlier, and more encouraging friends. May God richly bless each of you and your families.

Table of Contents

Introduction

THE PRIMARY GOAL of this book series is to establish the historical and social precedent that faith and religious practice are intrinsic to public life. Our religion is part of who we are, and we cannot check our minds, hearts, or souls at the door of the Capitol or office. Our life and work are built upon a theological and philosophical foundation. Whether we acknowledge it or not, we act based on certain moral presuppositions. This book makes the case that to understand how Christian leadership plays a prominent role in the United States of America we must look to the history of the church in Western Civilization. Christianity has had a marked effect on our modern world by instilling and bolstering our religious, social, and family life. Therefore, as a people, we must walk the line between religious adherence and legalism to maintain the proper place of the evangelical, fundamental, and the orthodox Christian church.

I hope that this book assists and guides our nation during this time of great moral confusion. We need to better understand the root of religion and how Christianity built the rational framework of Western Civilization. It is not meant to be an exhaustive treatment of every subject addressed. Dates *Before Christ* are listed as BC and dates *Anno Domini,* or AD, are displayed numerically. Approximate dates are assumed to be accurate enough unless otherwise noted. Occasionally, works cited are dated to their original publication rather than their reprinted date to maintain contiguity with the era and source. This is the first part of my summary of grand history in Western Civilization that will take place in four separate books. The first book, *The Constantine Doctrine,* concerns the foundation of religion spanning the ancient era through the Middles Ages. The second book, *The Columbus Initiative*, picks up with the Crusades and Age of Exploration through The First Great Awakening prior to the Declaration of Independence. The third book, *The Lincoln Legacy*, begins with the American Revolution and ends with World War II. The final installment, *The Reagan Compromise*, addresses our recent history beginning in the 1960s through present day. It is an integrated and synthetic sociological history rather than a chronological work. Ideas, people, and events from various eras are woven together while the thrust of the book tracks the linear progress of time from early proto-religion to the development of modern theology.

The Constantine Doctrine is meant to touch on some key ideas that have been explored in greater depth by many scholars and commentators. If you are interested in any of the ideas discussed, you will find various resources presented in the notes and references. You may start a conversation with friends and colleagues about any ideas that you agree or disagree with or reach out to me. This is the critical thinking and freedom of expression that I encourage and even demand in my classroom. Therefore, this book is part of a multivolume integrated historical survey that connects our past to the present. My goal is to show the consequences of the actions taken by fallible people which have led to this present situation in America.

The topic of Christian leadership in political, legal, military, and managerial positions will be addressed throughout the book. And while I would recommend that those Christians so inclined and called run for office and seek justice in our legal system, the point of this book is much broader than that. Christians seek to redeem the world through our witness and actions. We can do so in any walk of life, including and especially in public office, as well as in our businesses, work, and communities. We trust that when Jesus returns the governmental structures of this present age will fade away. Until then, we have a redemptive role to play in our everyday lives.

Christians have encouraged the growth of religious pluralism for hundreds of years. We typically advocate for the freedom of conscience and faith, regardless of the system of belief. We believe that the truth in God's word is more important than loyalty to any one group or cause. Because Christianity is true it will be effective in reforming the human condition spiritually and to a lesser degree physically. In America, we allow Judaism, Islam, Hinduism, Buddhism, Sikhism, and Zoroastrianism to be practiced alongside Catholic, Anglican, Lutheran, Baptist, Presbyterian, Methodist, and Non-denominational churches. The United States permitted and encouraged religious expressions even amid vehement debates and violent battles. We have set the standard for political liberty and religious freedom that many nations aspire to. This is part of Christian leadership.

All biblical quotations are from the English Standard Version (ESV) unless otherwise noted. The biblical references are included in the text rather than footnoted to provide direct citations of the scripture. Often the idea from the Bible will be prefaced with context to link it to the overall themes in the book. In some cases (often noted by a or b indicating the front or back selection) verses are shortened for readability or punctuation truncated and altered. While this is normally not the preferred approach to biblical references, it is necessary to maintain the flow of the narrative. Christians consider the Bible the Word of God inspired by the Holy Spirit. Academic articles or websites are footnoted, but this never indicates complete agreement with the source text. In academic writing, it is appropriate to acknowledge the role of researchers, scholars, and sources that we may not agree with in total, but which have certain points or historical facts that we can use. This practice can bolster the arguments in this book when other authors accept the same set of facts or have put forth similar theories.

To make the case for Christian leadership we must draw from a large interdisciplinary approach to Christian leadership, public policy, and governance. The sociology of religion is woven throughout this book without attempting to capture the debates, complexity, or nuance of the discipline. I will readily admit that this is not my area of expertise, I studied organizational leadership, but it is an area of interest. Again, this book is not meant to be exhaustive in its references or critique of various positions, histories of religions, or Christian traditions. I am leaving breadcrumbs that we may all follow. If you choose you may do some additional research and confirm or question my conclusions. I will certainly be following up with many arguments and ongoing research in this area.

While this book follows the arc of history, it is not purely chronological. Instead, this is a polemic teaching device meant to challenge, educate, and inform the reader. It is didactic in the sense that it teaches moral issues from a holistic, strategic, philosophical, and historical perspective. My extensive graduate and doctoral studies in leadership and business allow me to draw together interdisciplinary connections. I am not a historian by profession, but we all have an interest in history and leadership studies drawn from our collective past.

Each chapter merges historical precedent and a global perspective on religion with modern-day challenges and solutions to these entrenched problems. The shape of this book is as follows; it begins with a description of the era of conflict in which we live in Chapters 1, 2, and 3. We detail the lines between religions, secular movements, and sectarian violence. Reaching toward the reign of Constantine the groundwork is set for his eventual transformative leadership. In Chapters 4, 5, and 6 the religious and social nature of human beings is demonstrated showing how the state is linked to religion. Western Civilization is not the only civilization. Comparing various cultures and religions show how laws instantiate a moral code, regardless of the source of that morality. These laws either flow from natural law and conscience given to us by God or earthly ideas from kings, seers, philosophers, congressional representatives, academics, or judges. Humans have a God-shaped hole in their hearts, and this is expressed in how we govern. We either point people toward God or away from Him.

Then Chapters 7, 8, 9, and 10 outline the relationship between the church and state in the history of deistic representations of rulers. Humans have always deified their leaders, and we still do to some degree. Then, the Roman Empire took a turn with Constantine described in Chapters 11 and 12. As the first Christian head of state, he launched the European transformation from warring tribes into a warring nation-state. Christianity merged the Greco-Roman democracy with the Judeo legal structures instituting a government of law, led by flawed men, to build the kingdom of God. European Christianity is then explored as the outcropping of the Roman Church from Saint Augustine (354-430) to the Protestant Reformation. Augustine's City of God[1] is later compared to Abraham Kuyper's (1837-1920) ideas on sphere sovereignty.[2] In Chapters 16 and 17 "role

---

[1] Augustine. The City of God. (1903). United Kingdom: J. M. Dent.
[2] Kuyper, A. (2016). Pro Rege: Living Under Christ's Kingship (Volume 1). United Kingdom: Lexham Press.

of the Constantine Doctrine in the Dark and Middle Ages" is explained. We explain the role of the Constantine Doctrine in the Dark and Middle Ages leading to the Crusades and the clash between Islam and the church in Asia, Africa, and Europe.

I hope and pray that this effort serves you well. If so, it is only because of God's grace and provision. It is my sincere desire that we will experience a national revival and turn back toward the faith of our fathers and honor God. I believe that "if my people who are called by my name humble themselves and pray and seek my face and turn from their wicked ways, then I will hear from heaven and will forgive their sin and heal their land" (2 Chronicles 7:14). We still have a strong moral core linked to our Christian heritage; that beating heart of our national body may be injured but we can heal.

1

One Nation Under God

WHEN I RETURNED from Dubai, UAE, in 2020 after visiting Istanbul, Turkey, in 2019, I was struck by the way that religion is suffused throughout human life. The United Arab Emirates is a monarchy with a written constitution that provides numerous benefits to the citizens of the nation. While there are highly limited freedoms to resident guests, as a Muslim country it acknowledges its source of authority in the Islamic religion. It is nowhere near as free as the United States, but I became more aware of the efforts that have been made in the USA to suppress the religious aspect of who we are. In comparison, the UAE, an Islamic country, allows churches to meet when approved by government agencies. We cannot promote diversity of opinions while suppressing the views inherent in the Christian faith. Ronald Reagan (1911-2004) said that "freedom prospers when religion is vibrant and the rule of law under God is acknowledged."[3] This effort to remove Christianity from public life is the clearest violation of liberty and truth we have faced as a nation.

Rather than viewing the conflicts between the church and state as examples of a secular mandate to eradicate faith, we must work out this tension. The church led Western Civilization toward the very balance that the US has sought to achieve from its inception. But this balance has been lost. With constant

---

[3] Kriminger, J. (2020). The New Cold War: US-Russian Relations Under the Trump Administration (2017-2020). East Carolina University.

vigilance, good governance requires a moral populace and sound leadership that is best founded on the biblical and Christian worldview. We cannot separate faith and practice, especially in the formation and execution of our laws. To have a moral nation we must have moral guidance. This comes primarily from recognizing our dependence on God for salvation, the Bible as a historical, religious, and moral text as well as traditions that originate from the Christian faith. Christianity went from a small sect to a global movement as it spread from Jerusalem to Rome, London, and Philadelphia so that God could achieve his purpose in the redemption of many.

We must navigate this path as citizens in our government and society. By using authority as believing Christians, we do not acquiesce power to those who would take it nor seize power for personal gain. We should make common cause with all those who join us in this pursuit. If we can partner with nominal Christians, people of varied religions, or rational secularists who value moral traditions to better our world, so be it. We will return to this point repeatedly: America was never intended to be a theocracy but it was founded on the Christian religion so that people can come to know God. The church exists first and foremost to spread the gospel and bring God glory. Western Civilization has conflicted with other civilizations as well as engaged in internal battles over personal errors and inconsistencies in worldview. As George Santayana famously said, "Those who cannot remember the past are condemned to repeat it."[4] The Constantine Doctrine uses history to frame the experience

---

[4] Santayana, G. (2001). The Letters of George Santayana, Book Eight, 1948-1952 (Vol. 5). MitPress.

we have today and aids Christian leaders who seek to increase freedom and peace in this world.

An Example of Leadership

The Constantine Doctrine asserts that religion and governance are linked. Christians must take a prominent role in shaping policies and laws in the United States of America the same way that we led in the development of Europe. Historically, Christians in government leadership positions have benefited people throughout the globe, starting with Constantine in 306. Christians founded the United States of America specifically with the purpose of religious freedom as a guide toward political liberty which started with Constantine. Christians must fulfill this responsibility in our national discourse by guiding our nation and leading public policy. Christianity provides the single greatest framework and superstructure for a functional and free society. Ordering our government by instituting moral laws gives us the freedom to choose right or wrong actions and face the consequences of these actions. The Constantine Doctrine is the principle that any government will provide justice, support freedom, perform its duties well, and ensure prosperity when Christians take a prominent role in the leadership of that nation to encourage Christian leadership throughout the society.

With this effort, we may influence other nations of the world and learn from their culture which can incorporate the Christian faith. We have in the past. Our contributions to social progress, community organizations, healthy wellbeing, and international peace are profound. We laid the groundwork for an economic system that has produced amazing technological advances. All of this came with certain tradeoffs.

Christians should continue to take an active role in the government of our nation and the institutions and organizations that shape our culture, society, and civilization. The protections afforded religion in the first amendment of the Bill of Rights and subsequent legislation apply to Christianity as much if not more than any other religion. Christians have had an instrumental part to play in our progress from colonies into a nation. We have led during trying seasons and should feel compelled to do so at every opportunity. The church cannot shirk its responsibility to lead and influence our nation and this world for the good to the glory of God.

The Constantine Doctrine includes a critique of Christianity and Christians as much as it is an endorsement of the belief systems that undergirds our Western Civilization. We have failed in many ways. Sinful people claiming the name of Jesus Christ have perpetrated numerous evils on the world. But as Joseph said to his brothers, "As for you, you meant evil against me, but God meant it for good" (Genesis 50:20). Individual failures do not negate God's sovereign plan. And this book is a call for spiritual revival not just culturally and socially but on a personal level. We need God more now than ever. We must obey scripture, "Do not be conformed to this world, but be transformed by the renewal of your mind, that by testing you may discern what is the will of God, what is good and acceptable and perfect" (Romans 12:2). Our friends and neighbors may turn to embrace the truths of scripture as we conform our minds according to God's will.

Two questions frame this discussion. What actions honor God to strengthen the church and which ones compromise our witness? Many Christians accuse others of damaging the brand of the church by supporting people who are not orthodox or pure. We must not compromise our principles and practice

God's grace and truth. Did Jesus violate his principles when he reached out to the least and lost? "The Son of Man came eating and drinking, and they say, 'Here is a glutton and a drunkard, a friend of tax collectors and sinners.' But wisdom is proved right by her deeds" (Matthew 11:19). There is a difference between the policies we support to promote a Christian worldview and the deeds of any one individual. We meet people where they are, whether in the homeless shelter or boardroom. The question then becomes, is that person qualified to lead based on their own life, shortcomings, and skills?

A Point of Comparison

In Dubai, the Muslim call to prayer *salat* is heard throughout the city five times a day. Ramadan is a holiday that is practiced with devotion and excitement for the *Iftar* (evening meal), *Ishtar* (morning meal), and *Eid al-Fitr* (final day, festival breaking the fast). A *Hajj* (religious pilgrimage) is considered a legitimate thirty-day employee leave that is legally granted and honored by all employers.[5] Religious aspects of life are supported by the laws of the land in this country. For example, banking laws adhere to Islamic Shari'a, according to the UAE website:

> The UAE offers Islamic banking services. It is governed by Shari'a law and Federal Law No. 6 of 1985 regarding Islamic banks, financial institutions and investment companies. According to Article 3 of the law, Islamic banks have the right to carry on all or part of banking, commercial, financial and investment services and

---

[5] https://www.emirates247.com/news/emirates/what-are-the-leave-and-holiday-entitlements-for-uae-employees-2012-10-09-1.478386

operations. They have the right to engage in all types of services and operations practiced by banks and referred to in Federal Law No. 10 of 1980. In October 2013, H.H. Sheikh Mohammed bin Rashid Al Maktoum launched a strategic plan for developing the Islamic economy sector. The plan includes 7 key pillars and 46 strategic initiatives. One of the initiatives is the establishment of Islamic banking center in Dubai.[6]

There are no equivalent Christian banking systems or laws in the US. Western culture has struggled to come to terms with the concept of charging interest, often referred to as usury in religious literature, and managing debt. Short-term or payday loans have rates equivalent to a loan shark, and yet some scholars make the case for high-interest loans to establish credit in the lower class among other liquidity benefits.[7] But there are significant downside risks and costs that lock in cycles of poverty for many underprivileged communities. We allow and even encourage bankruptcy as a way to protect entrepreneurs.[8] We strap students with massive student loans, underwritten by the federal government.[9] The financial crisis of 2008 started with the government incentivizing no-documentation loans for individuals to exceed standard liability guides on home purchases.[10]

---

[6] https://u.ae/en/information-and-services/finance-and-investment/banking

[7] Skiba, P. M. (2012). Regulation of payday loans: Misguided. Wash. & Lee L. Rev., 69, 1023.

[8] Skiba, P. M., & Tobacman, J. (2019). Do payday loans cause bankruptcy?. The Journal of Law and Economics, 62(3), 485-519.

[9] Ratcliffe, C., & McKernan, S. M. (2013). Forever in your debt: Who has student loan debt, and who's worried. Washington, DC: Urban Institute.

[10] Acharya, V. V., & Richardson, M. (2009). Causes of the financial crisis. Critical review, 21(2-3), 195-210.

This was accelerated by fraudulent mortgage brokers who lied on applications to corporate executives who manipulated their reports and knowingly sold worthless assets to other banks endangering our whole economy.[11] Then these banks claimed that they were "too big to fail" and that the federal government must bail them out, which it did.

So, instead of any moral guidance on lending, we have banking regulations such as the 2002 Sarbanes-Oxley Act.[12] For the most part, banks are secular profit-seeking firms.[13] But we can see how well their codes of ethics worked out in 2008 with the financial crisis they created. In comparison, there is a debate in the UAE about the role of Islamic banking. Some believe that this concept is just a way to conduct the same practices of lending and credit using religious terminology. However, there are clear differences between the USA and UAE related to religion and ethics linked to the practice of banking. This is not a recommendation to adopt Islamic standards in banking, quite the contrary, it is a recognition of the important role that religion plays in all aspects of our lives, including finances. Overarching standards of ethics must guide the use of our finances and permeate our laws. In western nations, the basis of law is the Christian religion.

And this is just one industry. Banking may be a key component of our economic activity however as the heart-pumping lifeblood of capital throughout the economy, damage to the heart imperils the entire body. More to the point, unethical business

---

[11] Jickling, M. (2009). Causes of the financial crisis.

[12] https://www.congress.gov/bill/107th-congress/house-bill/3763

[13] Yaniv Roznai citing Domenic Marbaniang in "Negotiating the Eternal: The Paradox of Entrenching Secularism in Constitutions", Michigan State Law Review 253, 2017, p. 324

practices are like an infection in our system. Religion is a vital part of life in the UAE, from employment law and banking to daily activities, and meals. It is used as a touchstone for families. Religion is not viewed as a building location or holiday debate about decorations, it is a core and central aspect of national unity. The same was once said of America.

The Political Spectrum

Understanding religion and government in America starts with distinguishing between the positions of the various parties and factions in this nation. Our present problems stem from past arguments expanded on in *The Columbus Initiative*, the next book in this series. There are both religious and political divisions in this country's past and present. The divisiveness that stems from religious differences mirrors political fighting. Local churches in America have separated because of doctrinal disputes or personal differences between pastors or congregations. What starts as minor infighting and squabbles become larger problems often between people who want to change and those who want to maintain the status quo. Separation in churches may come from church discipline, a lack of magnanimity, or the failure of negotiations. Similarly, we have refought political battles drawn on lines of what is presently called conservatism and liberalism, the right and the left of the political spectrum respectively.

We can draw this spectrum in terms of policies favoring tradition versus change or we can describe it in terms of the desire for control versus freedom. The origin of the political labels left and right was the seating of members of the French Parliament based on the institutions (aristocracy and church) on the right and rising commoner capitalists on the left.[14] Edmund Burke (1729-1797) observed that the roots of the French Revolution were in the decay of the Divine right of Kings and the Church, corruption of the fiscal system, mistaken economic principles, growth of philosophies (those atheistic ideas), and theories of State which consolidate power in the hands of a few.[15] This has become the conservative critique of revolution. Change may be for the better, but it often is not. This is the principle of "Chesterton's Fence." Rather than change for the sake of change, think about why the fence exists before you remove it. "If you don't see the use of it, I certainly won't let you clear it away. Go away and think. Then, when you can come back and tell me that you do see the use of it, I may allow you to destroy it."[16]

Before America, monarchists favored government and reformers favored individual liberty. Since the formation of the USA, this distinction fails to set the boundaries of freedom and limitations on individual rights, because progressives have attempted to reform society through the state. A tradition that provides law and order moderates the desire for freedom in all aspects of our lives and the desire for control by aristocratic elitists. Therefore, we must ask what type of laws are needed? The dimension of control versus freedom does not define the nature of an ordered state. Both parties in America, Democrats on the left and Republicans on the right, support some freedoms and some controls. Christian leaders can help us reach an appropriate balance.

---

[14] Knapp, Andrew; Wright, Vincent (2006). "1 French political traditions in a changing context" (ebk). The Government and Politics of France (5 ed.). Taylor and Francis.
[15] Burke, E. (1790). Reflections on the French revolution (Vol. 460). CUP Archive.
[16] Chesterton, G. K. (1929). The thing. Aeterna Press.

Many attempts to capture differences in human orientation toward government have been made. All have been criticized. Some are more helpful than others. But each reflects the presuppositions of the researcher. This framework will be helpful moving forward as references on political positions are made. In 1941, Leonard W. Ferguson (1912-1988), an American Psychologist, developed the first political attitudes survey that measured opinions on birth control, capital punishment, censorship, communism, evolution, law, patriotism, theism, criminality, and war and, with factor analysis, identified three factors he called humanitarianism, religionism, and nationalism.[17] A multivariate factor analysis simply shows which answers to a group of questions move in the same direction or "hang together."[18] Later, Hans Esyenck (1916-1997), a German-British social scientist, described political attitudes on bipolar scales of change (radical versus conservative) and government (authoritarian versus democratic).[19] Milton Rokeach (1918-1988) developed another model based on regard for freedom and equality.[20] Ronald Inglehart (1934-2021) and other researchers have gathered data from the World Values Survey and extrapolated two scales, traditionalist versus secular and self-expression versus survivalist.[21] In 2007, Brian Patrick Mitchell (b. 1960?) published his work on Anglo-American political thought offering his model based on rank (*archy*, or anarchy versus hierarchy) versus force (*kratos* versus *akreteia*) which he linked to the relationship

---

[17] Ferguson, L.W. (1941). "The Stability of the Primary Social Attitudes: I. Religionism and Humanitarianism". Journal of Psychology. 12 (2): 283–8.
[18] Brown, T. A. (2015). Confirmatory factor analysis for applied research. Guilford publications.
[19] Eysenck, H. J. (1956). Sense and Nonsense in Psychology. Pelican.
[20] Rokeach, Milton (1973). The nature of human values. Free Press.
[21] Inglehart, R. (2015). Inglehart–Welzel cultural map. World Values Survey.

between the church and state.[22] Views on religion affect votes and public policy.

Supposedly, in America, we have two parties that represent differing views. In terms of religious practice, Christians tend to support the Republican party. However, a large contingent of Republicans is nominally religious and entertains the use of secular state power for special interests. Debates about the Religious Right are addressed in *The Reagan Compromise,* the last book in this series that addresses modern American religion and politics. The liberal Democrat party has an anti-religious ideology that dovetails with aspects of European socialism. This view supports atheism, multiculturalism, pagan religions, and Islam which acts as a foil against the evangelical and fundamentalist Christians in the more conservative Republican Party.[23] At the same time, the Democrat party has received substantial votes from many Catholic, Jewish, liberal mainline Protestant, and African-American religious communities. These divisions cross denominations and are rooted in ancient differences connected to disagreements about tradition versus change as well as control versus freedom.

Secular ideology motivates with the same vigor as a religious movement. In America today, Democrats are on the left and favor governmental control, not unlike those used in the UAE and China, with more libertine social and cultural changes found in Europe. While the Republicans are on the right and prefer local authority, individual rights, the rule of law, and political liberty.

[22] Mitchell, Brian Patrick (2007). Eight ways to run the country: a new and revealing look at left and right. Greenwood Publishing.
[23] Cliteur, P., & Ellian, A. (2020). The Five Models for State and Religion: Atheism, Theocracy, State Church, Multiculturalism, and Secularism. ICL Journal.

However, corrupt, and immoral Republicans and Democrats oppose religion and personal accountability as they vie for and use power. Therefore, the positions of parties on religion have little to do with the vicissitudes of electoral politics. Many of these politicians are compromised and use the cloak of religion as a mask to cover their criminal ambitions. Our public discourse on religion in the USA has moved leftward. In America, we have amputated the expression of our souls. Compare that to the UAE, where a public call to prayer is normal. In the USA, people are sued for practicing their faith when they say a prayer at work.

Threats to Public Faith

A judge at the local and appellate level in the Second Circuit court ruled against Christians who prayed in public. Only when it was heard at the US Supreme Court was the previous ruling overturned and religious practice upheld.[24] In the *Town of Greece v. Galloway, 572 U.S. 565* (2014) two plaintiffs, Susan Galloway and Linda Stephens, represented by Americans United for Separation of Church and State sued the town of Greece, NY, for allowing chaplains to pray in public to open a meeting.[25] The Supreme Court ruled in favor of the defendant and supported the right of people to pray. It found that this practice is appropriate and aligned with America's tradition. Voluntary prayer in the town meeting did not force atheists to participate in prayer but acknowledged our heritage and foundation for a just society. In contrast, the UAE encourages Muslims to pray and practice religious activities, it requires businesses and government agencies

---

[24] Town of Greece v. Galloway, No. 12-696, 572 U.S. (2014).
[25] Bennett, Daniel (2017). Defending Faith: The Politics of the Christian Conservative Legal Movement. University Press of Kansas. ISBN 978-0700624607.

to abide by these traditions but does not force non-Muslims to follow the same requirements. Alcohol is banned in Sharjah, the emirate north of Dubai but allowed in Dubai. Compare the old Blue Laws in the USA to Ramadan in the UAE. We used to limit sales on the Sabbath, one day a week, while the Emirates restrict the sale and display of food in public during a holy month of fasting to reduce the temptation for practicing Muslims as a sign of respect.

Our legal battles are constantly renewed as individuals are attacked for practicing their God-given rights of faith and speech in this nation. When we think about the freedom America affords its citizens, we must acknowledge that these rights are being challenged by a vocal and adamant minority of our population who are opposed to religion. We cannot allow our faith to hang in the balance by capricious judges. Christianity and other religions are allowed in Dubai. This level of religious pluralism was nearly unheard of in the Muslim world seventy or even twenty years ago. Yet, more nations in the Middle East are following the lead of the UAE. Building a faith community of ex-pats is even encouraged because the nation recognizes the value of religious expression in the lives of the residents in the country. The story of Christianity in the UAE is one of love and generosity tied to freedom, compassion, and faith.

Jesus and the gospel are alive and well in the UAE even though the proselytization of Muslims is expressly forbidden by law. Various Christian denominations, sects, and theologies vie for the attention of many residents. The fact that the UAE is open to many religions is highly significant. Conversations about God and faith are openly allowed. Many of the casual phrases used by Muslims carry a religious connotation. *Inshallah* is a very frequent utterance referring to our inability to make commitments apart from God's decree, it means "if Allah wills it." *Alhamdulillah* is a common answer to the question "How are you," it means "praise to Allah" and is used to express gratitude. *Mashallah* is a congratulatory phrase that means "as Allah has willed." This is not to say that every expression is meant to express devotion. These are often simply colloquial phrases, but they carry the culture the way that "God bless you" and "Thank God" used to in America. Do the words of Christians mean what we say? Islam as a political force in the Middle Ages is addressed in later chapters and more recently in *The Reagan Compromise*. While it is important to acknowledge the cultural aspects of religious language, the origin of many phrases is theistic.

On the contrary, as these words have become distanced from their original meaning, they are still meant to preserve a semblance of religious observation. In the UAE, the total population is nearly 9.8 million people (Emirati and residents). Demographically, 76 percent are Muslim, 9 percent are Christian, and 15 percent have various other religious beliefs.[26] There are Jews, Hindus, Buddhists, Parsis, Baha'is, Druze, and Sikhs residing, working, and openly worshiping in the country. The Pew Research Center estimated that in 2010, "76.9 percent of the total population was Muslim, 12.6 percent Christian, 6.6 percent Hindu, 2 percent Buddhist, with the remaining belonging to other faith traditions."[27] In a monarchial nation that is rated 17/100 as "not free" in general electoral freedom by the Freedom House, a research corporation founded by Raymond Gastil

---

[26] https://u.ae/en/information-and-services/social-affairs
[27] https://www.state.gov/reports/2018-report-on-international-religious-freedom/united-arab-emirates

(1931-2010), religion is openly practiced.[28] Compare that to the experience of Christians in America over the last fifty years.

Christian churches in the USA meet within certain limitations such as land use, tax exemption, meeting times, and locations. However, non-Christian religion in America broadly defined is allowed and even encouraged as in the case of Islam.[29] The conditions for religious practice and its effect on public policy have been reduced in America and expanded in the Emirates. This can only be because of the intention of certain leaders in our respective nations. Our culture and society both mirror and shape our laws and public policy. American laws should support our Christian heritage because it provides the most clearly shared national identity.

---

[28] https://freedomhouse.org/
[29] https://freedomhouse.org/

2

Leadership in the UAE and America

COMPARING THE ROLE of leaders requires a brief synopsis of leadership in the UAE. This nation has undergone an amazing transition from tribalism and religious intolerance to openness and economic opportunity. This change is reflected in the recent efforts to establish diplomatic and trade relations between Muslim and Jewish nations. Leadership is the key to unlocking the shared purposes of individuals. Ethical leadership is a category of leadership rather than a distinct theory of leadership.[30] It incorporates ethics into leadership. Ethics are standards for human behavior, what we ought to do, which act as a plumbline for all organizational and professional roles. Engineers, teachers, bus drivers, executives, and politicians are all judged based on ethical standards. Efforts led by the US administration with strong ties to the evangelical Christian community, favorable to more moderate Islamic countries, and overly supportive of Israel, show the way that ethical leadership can be transformational.

A landmark peace agreement, called the Abraham Accords, established between the Muslim nations of the UAE (Sunni) and Bahrain (Shia), and Israel, brokered by the USA under President Donald Trump demonstrates the fact that religion does not

---

[30] Darville, Yoon (2020), Implementation of CEO Servant Leadership: From Research Into Practice by Exploring Roles of CEO Servant Leadership in American For-Profit Organizations. Multidisciplinary Perspectives on Managerial and Leadership Psychology. Ed. Rick Johnson.

have to be a dividing line in the Middle East. In many ways, a Christian work ethic, liberties, personal responsibility, and free-market economics have spanned the gaps between cultures in our world. This outreach can be done wisely or poorly. If the goal is peace, then trade and commerce are prerequisites. With the effort spearheaded by Jared Kushner (b. 1981), the husband of Trump's daughter Ivanka and a Modern Orthodox Jew, the members of this agreement showed their willingness to work together. This amount of cooperation provides hope for future relationships in the region.

As the fountainhead of monotheism, the Middle East has a history of warfare and conquest. But, by the grace of God, certain Christians felt called to minister to the Arab people of this remote peninsula to relieve the suffering that many families had endured for generations. Stories we read are told by the people who survived, but many never made it out of childhood and their stories were never written. Such was the case in the Trucial States, a British name for the confederation of tribes under their protection along the Persian Gulf. The UAE was the brainchild of Sheik Zayed bin Sultan Al Nahyan (1918-2004). A nation birthed in a harsh environment that became an economic powerhouse through peace and tolerance.[31] Leadership must incorporate the shared purpose of various people. Christians have often helped to improve the living conditions in nations as an evangelical tool. We cannot share the gospel with people who struggle with warfare, gaining potable water, and the lack of food and other necessities. The UAE would not exist if there

---

[31] Edward Henderson (1988), This strange eventful history, London: Quartet Books,

were not enough people and families to bring Nahyan's vision to fruition.

Al Nahyan presents a case study in leadership. His vision for the Emirate tribes in the Western portion of Arabia during the 1970s was compelling.[32] His ability to gain and rally support to build a coalition from disparate family leaders was astounding considering the past fighting and bad blood in the region.[33] He had a keen and curious intellect with a charismatic and compassionate personality. Leadership literature has attempted varied explanations of how leaders emerge or gain support. This area of research is linked to the way that leaders are identified and mature.[34] However, the prevailing answer to the question of whether leaders are born or made? is that leaders are both born and made. Yet the way that one leads is connected to their style and the effectiveness of that person is correlated with their opportunities to learn and the demands of the situations they face. Looking back on archival evidence, Sheik Zayed has many of the attributes of ethical and charismatic leadership and behaved according to Servant Leadership.[35] Recognizing the impact of his leadership highlights the practical ways the influence relationship between leaders and followers affects nations. He was open to the best advice from experts in any field.

---

[32] Yakheek, M. M. (2003). Strategic Vision of His Highness Sheikh Zayed Bin Sultan Al Nahyan. Army War College, Carlisle PA.

[33] Alhosani, H. A. (2012). The Political Thought of the Late HH Sheikh Zayed Bin Sultan Al Nahyan, Founder of the United Arab Emirates (1966-2004) (Doctoral dissertation, Durham University).

[34] Zaccaro, S. J. (2007). Trait-based perspectives of leadership. American psychologist, 62(1), 6.

[35] Al Fahim, M. (1995). From rags to riches. Dubai, UAE: London Centre of Arab Studies.

Dr. Pat Kennedy, house call 1970.

Marian and Pat Kennedy were Christian missionaries who founded the Oasis Hospital in Al Ain in November 1960. Sheik Zayed bin Sultan Al Nahyan invited the couple to help the people in the region.[36] Al Nahyan was the ruling governor of this city in the emirate of Abu Dhabi before his instrumental work in founding the nation of the UAE in 1971. Al Ain had an excessive infant and maternal mortality rate. One in three mothers died and only half of the babies survived. Disease and infections were poorly treated. The Kennedys provided for the physical and spiritual needs of people who had very different religious beliefs than themselves.

The Kennedys demonstrate the model of Servant Leadership that Jesus Christ exemplified and taught to his disciples. Servant

---

[36] "Oasis Hospital celebrates 50 years of care for a community". The National. June 27, 2010.

Leadership balances leading while serving.[37] It is an approach to leadership that emphasizes ethics, human development, and organizational purpose. Servant Leadership finds its clearest expression by Jesus: "Whoever wants to become great among you must be your servant, and whoever wants to be first must be servant of all. For even the Son of Man did not come to be served, but to serve, and to give his life as a ransom for many (Mark 10:42-45)." This partnership between Christian doctors and a Muslim prince demonstrates a path to reach humanitarian goals.

They were later joined by other Christian missionaries from the US and Canada. The hospital started as a mud hut, they built a cement building in 1964 and in 1972 added an X-ray, a maternity delivery suite, and other facilities. By 1985, pediatrics, surgery, and obstetrics were added. The Oasis Hospital was acquired by CURE International in 2006.[38] In 2009, $36.45 million was invested as grant-in-aid constructing a 200-bed hospital and twenty-eight NICU beds and seven ICUs. CEO David Printy noted, "We are the only hospital we know of that does not refuse patients" due to donations from local Emiratis. Nancy Brock worked as a nurse in the Oasis Hospital for thirty-five years. She said, "I loved my job and Arab hospitality meant I often had coffee and dried dates with them while I was teaching patients. I was also invited to homes frequently, especially if I had delivered a baby in the family. We were a part of the community."[39] This level of integration with the local community is an example of the effective use of medical

---

[37] Darville, Yoon, & Spann. (2020). A Literature Review of CEO Servant Leadership and Social Responsibility in American For-Profit Organizations. Multidisciplinary Perspectives on Managerial and Leadership Psychology. Ed. Rick Johnson

[38] https://cure.org/united-arab-emirates/

[39] https://www.thenational.ae/uae/health/how-missionaries-transformed-abu-dhabi-healthcare-1.482263

missions to open doors for future Christians to walk through. The priority is the care of the people to show them the love of Christ.

While overt efforts to convert Muslims are prohibited, evangelical churches can exist in Dubai with permission to operate and witness. This religious openness has blessed the people of this state with peace and prosperity. The practice of Islam is not primarily responsible for the success of the UAE, many nations are Islamic by law. Oil and trade certainly played a bigger part in the stratospheric growth of this small nation than any other economic factor. Yet in addition to economic factors, leadership and the tolerance for other belief systems has played a significant part in welcoming people of varied faiths and practice to the UAE. I have heard it said by Muslims and Christians that God has blessed this nation with leadership, vision, and wealth. The variety and diversity of many belief systems are a blessing. This permissive atmosphere is a stark contrast to the attacks on religious expressions in America and especially the assault on Christian leadership that we face. The way that Islam is celebrated in the Emirates is how Christianity was once revered in the States. Church bells ringing in small towns across America were as ubiquitous as the call to prayer is in a futuristic city like Dubai.

American Religious Practice

To contrast the religious aspects and leadership of the UAE with that of the US consider the practice of holiday observations. The word holiday, from Holy Day, is suffused with religious connotations even as the experience of many lack religious fealty and have become more commercialized.[40] Christmas is the

---

[40] McCrossen, A. (2001). Holy Day, Holiday: The American Sunday. Cornell University Press.

most popular holiday in this country. The original name comes from the religious service, mass, celebrating Jesus' miraculous virgin birth. While the exact date of his birth may be unknown, the Julian calendar is benchmarked to the year 0 BC, Before Christ.[41] Modern public school students have been taught to use the abbreviation BCE which stands for Before Common Era, in an attempt to rewrite history.[42] Easter is the holiest day in the Christian calendar. On this day, we celebrate Jesus' resurrection and our new birth. This historical fact stands out among religious ceremonies; no other religious figure claimed to be God and was raised by God from the dead.[43] It is a running joke that some people only attend church on Christmas and Easter. After the COVID-19 pandemic of 2020 locked down many buildings, even these events will become inconvenient for most Americans.

How has America strayed so far from its founding? This is developed here and addressed more fully in *The Columbus Initiative* and *The Lincoln Legacy*. We can learn from a small Muslim country like the UAE about the role that religion plays in our daily lives. In many ways, we once protected expressions of faith the way that other nations do now. We honored God with laws that preserved the practice of worship on Sunday. Once we esteemed God with our prayers and government and disparaged the use of vulgar language. Our national motto is "In God we trust." It was understood at our founding that "He has favored our undertakings" in Latin the maxim was written "*Novus ordo*

---

[41] Nissenbaum, S. (1997). The battle for Christmas. Vintage.

[42] Richards, E. G. (2012). "Calendars" (PDF). In Urban, S. E.; Seidelmann, P. K. (eds.). Explanatory Supplement to the Astronomical Almanac (3rd ed.). Mill Valley, CA: University Science Books. p. 585.

[43] Habermas, G. R. (2003). The risen Jesus & future hope. Rowman & Littlefield.

seclorum."[44] And our pledge of allegiance declares that we are "one nation under God."[45] These ideas have been leached of their meaning. Now, Christians are shamed and threatened when we pray, share our faith, and use biblical wisdom to make important decisions. Many people view religion as a tradition of the past and misconstrue science with methodological naturalism only giving a passing acknowledgment of spiritual and supernatural concerns in our lives.[46] Some scholars go as far as mistaking the supernatural basis of an ordered science rooted in metaphysics as conformity to superstition and bigotry.[47] Now singing the national anthem is controversial.

American Religious Foundations

Let us stipulate that enough Americans want to recover our foundational principles which guide our cultural and religious freedoms. Enough people are defined as the smallest group needed to begin and sustain a revival or movement. The Sons of Liberty founded by Samuel Adams (1722-1803) was based on the Loyal Nine. This small group became a kernel of the patriot cause which by 1775 added around 40 percent of colonists

---

[44] Caldwell, L. K. (1976). Novus ordo seclorum: The heritage of American public administration. Public Administration Review, 36(5), 476-488.

[45] Snake, R. (1961). One Nation Under God. R. G. Smith (Ed.). Wilfred Funk Incorporated.

[46] Mahner, M. (2012). The role of metaphysical naturalism in science. Science & Education, 21(10), 1437-1459.

[47] Kahn, L. (1918). Metaphysics of the Supernatural as Illustrated by Descartes. United States: Columbia University Press attempted but failed to refute History of Atomism from the Middle Ages to Newton translated K. Lasswitz's Geschichte der Atomistik vom Mittelalter bis Newton (2 vols., Leipzig, 1890). Philosophische Monatshefte 27: 334.

who supported the revolution.[48] From nine men, lawyers and businessmen, a nation grew. This fact is developed further in *The Columbus Initiative*. Christians as members of the church should appreciate how our religion has impacted world history and will affect the future of our civilization. How do we foster our Christian heritage and use these guideposts to positively impact our nation for God's glory? That is the primary question that drove my research in this text.

Christians should lead in all areas of our country, and work with people of all faiths in this leadership. This does not require strictly religious leaders in our nation or pursuing a theocracy. Leadership is a relationship between people. We must strive for a more righteous and ethical government. Labeling overt and unapologetic Christians who seek to be involved in charting the course of the United States as "theocrats" or "dominion-ists" is foolish. Most Christians have never read Rushdoony's *Institutes of Christian Law* and would not attempt to prosecute Old Testament crimes under our modern system of jurisprudence.[49] The accusation of an attempted Christian takeover of a nation founded by Christians is a non sequitur and meant to silence the church's witness. Sara Diamond (b. 1958) coined the term dominion as a neologism to describe the "central unifying ideology for the Christian."[50] This is false. Ross Douthat (b. 1979), a Catholic and conservative writer for the New York Times, wrote, "Many of the people that writers like Diamond

---

[48] Robert M. Calhoon, "Loyalism and neutrality" in Jack P. Greene; J. R. Pole (2008). A Companion to the American Revolution. John Wiley & Sons. p. 235.

[49] Rushdoony, R. J. (2009). The Institutes of Biblical Law Vol. 1 (Vol. 1). Chalcedon Foundation.

[50] Diamond, S. (1995). Roads to dominion: Right-wing movements and political power in the United States. Guilford Press.

and others describe as 'dominionists' would disavow the label, many definitions of dominionism conflate several very different Christian political theologies, and there's a lively debate about whether the term is even useful at all."[51]

According to these authors, there is a Christian around every corner hatching a plot. Religious journals have attempted to debunk these fears. *First Things* is an "educational institute aiming to advance a religiously informed public philosophy."[52] Editor Jeremy Pierce called the conspiracy theorists who fear theocracy "*dominionismists*."[53] Bruce Barron wrote, "Reconstructionists have many more sympathizers who fall somewhere within the dominionist framework, but who are not card-carrying members."[54] This McCarthyism veiled an attempt to label Christians who exert influence in public policy and culture as vile as Communists, the most prominent card issuing political movement in American history. Further, these authors associate Christians who participate in democracy with a cultic movement.

Charges that Christians are attempting to subjugate the population of America are especially offensive to people who tend toward free-market economics and generally reject cults as a matter of doctrine. Even if many of the views of Rushdoony on Christian reconstruction are valid and orthodox, the portion of

---

[51] Douthat, Ross 2011. "The New Yorker and Francis Schaeffer." The New York Times. August 29, 2011.

[52] https://www.firstthings.com/

[53] McVicar, M. J. (2013). "Let them have Dominion":"Dominion Theology" and the Construction of Religious Extremism in the US Media. The Journal of Religion and Popular Culture, 25(1), 120-145.

[54] Bruce Barron and Anson Shupe, 1992, "Reasons for the Growing Popularity of Christian Reconstructionism: The Determination to Attain Dominion", in Bronislaw Misztal and Anson D. Shupe, eds. Religion and politics in comparative perspective: revival of religious fundamentalism in East and West. Westport, Conn: Praeger.

his proposed plan that is impractical outweighs the benefits of adopting his philosophy wholesale. However, rather than recognizing his contribution to Christianity, he is cast aside because affiliating with him becomes akin to advocating for theocracy according to enemies of the church. You can see how the academic's move to create distance between the bulk of liberal mainline denominations and their secular brethren ostracized more fundamental Christians.

Christian theology, philosophy, and politics represent separate but related spheres of knowledge and influence. We worship, think, and act according to a coherent worldview that is both eternal in scope and temporal in application. Human dominion over the earth is part of God's design. Christians who lead efforts to increase righteousness and salvation are also part of God's plan. We get to participate in both. Specifically, in America we think, speak, and behave according to our beliefs, especially those rooted in the Christian faith.

America's Religious Heritage

This nation was founded on religious freedom. This topic makes up the bulk of *The Columbus Initiative*. Puritans fled persecution in Europe to make a living in a New World. Of course, these men and women suffered in a difficult land and had conflicts with other nationalities, the Native Indian tribes, and even different denominations. But what their descendents eventually accomplished in 1776 and 1789 was to promote a higher standard of government rooted in the Christian faith. The fact that nearly every nation in this world has adopted some version of a constitution (regardless of the type or form this document takes) is a testament to the lasting impact of the American Revolution. We believe that the written word can contain self-evident truths like the Bible does. The idea that a piece of paper could encapsulate the function of government is a unique gift to human development made by American Christians.

As we trace the role of religion in public life the God of history seems to funnel Christianity into the United States, where it once flourished. Then, the same God who preserved His church through the Middle Ages and wars used his people in positions of power to blunt evil and spread freedom during the twentieth century. America's participation in World Wars I and II to the Cold War was God's prevenient grace that dulled the advance of genocidal and atheistic regimes. The church had to persevere through famine, war, and division so that America would exist in the Twentieth Century. Over time this Christian ethic withered in our homeland, whether due to a lack of care or entropy. During the timeframe following World War II, the church became a less effective witness for Christ. This is the topic of *The Reagan Compromise*. Our collective history as followers of Christ sets our expectations for the future. We are left asking, what should we do now? We are to suffer well, serve fully, fight justly, and seek God completely.

Persecution and justice are both to be fully expected when serving God. Jesus said, "You will be hated by everyone because of me, but the one who stands firm to the end will be saved" (Matthew 10:22). Jesus did not say that he required us to be persecuted to be found faithful. Martyrdom is not a require-ment for the Christian, just like the gifts of the spirit or formal ministry are not normative experiences for every believer. But every follower of Christ should bear witness and be willing to stand on the truths of God no matter what.[55] Instead, we should expect that because we are faithful, we will run into opposition. Ironically, many people hate Christians because we preach the forgiveness of sin. This is because, to be forgiven of sin, you must first acknowledge that you are a sinner.

How we handle that opposition must be morally acceptable to the Lord. We are called to fight a good fight, in our professions, courts, public squares, and battlefields. This is firstly spiritual, but not only spiritual, "Fight the good fight of the faith. Take hold of the eternal life to which you were called and about which you made the good confession in the presence of many witnesses"(1 Timothy 6:12). Christians advocate for the truth and should debate the value of certain policies and positions that adhere to the truth. Apologetics is the defense of the Christian faith, not only theologically or philosophically but practically. In modern American society, any testimony may be greeted with a bevy of questions, "But sanctify the Lord God in your hearts and be ready always to give an answer to every man who asks you a reason for the hope that is in you, with meekness and fear" (1 Peter 3:15). We believe in objective truth rather than relativism. So, many of our conversations are precursors to the necessary resolution to these disagreements.

Meekness is not weakness, shyness, or timidity. Meekness is strength under control. "Blessed are the meek, for they shall inherit the earth" (Matthew 5:5). We know that *si vis pacem, para bellum*, "If you want peace, prepare for war"[56] and we should seek

---

[55] DeYoung, R. (2012). Courage. In Austin, M. W., & Geivett, R. D. (Eds.). (2011). Being good: Christian virtues for everyday life. Wm. B. Eerdmans Publishing.

[56] Book 3. Publius Flavius Vegetius Renatus. De Re Militari (~400 BC).

"peace through our strength" as Reagan put it.[57] If we cannot resolve our disagreements with a hostile power that attacks us, we will defend our rights and freedom. Since God endorsed self-defense and open warfare in the Old Testament, we should expect that service in the military of a just nation is an honorable profession. Jesus said to his disciples, "But now if you have a purse, take it, and also a bag; and if you don't have a sword, sell your cloak and buy one" (Luke 22:36). He expected them to use it. Jesus recommends taking proper precautions and did not speak against the Roman centurion's military role (see: Matthew 8). As *The Lincoln Legacy* details, faith was an essential part of our victories in World War I and II. Many American soldiers, sailors, and Marines have found great strength in the gospel. Now, we need more religion, not less, in our armed forces.

Alexis De Tocqueville wrote that "the greatness of America lies not in being more enlightened than any other nation, but rather in her ability to repair her faults."[58] This rings true, throughout our existence America has been a beacon of hope and freedom while providing a moral compass in our international policies. Our errors stem from our human failings. We have fought, bled, and died to make this a more perfect union aligned with our original mission statement in the Declaration of Independence. This is outlined in *The Columbus Initiative*. Our faith reaches back through time bringing with it a heritage of truth and order. We believe in God because He is real and active in this world. God gave us our reason with which we could fashion a civilization that honors and glorifies him amid this chaotic and vicious world. From the Judeo-Christian

---

[57] https://www.reaganlibrary.gov/permanent-exhibits/peace-through-strength
[58] De Tocqueville, A. (1835). Democracy in America.

ethic, the Greco-Roman polity, the European Reformation, Enlightenment, and scientific theories, a nation was formed that sought to balance the human needs for freedom and order.

3

America's Present Challenge

THE HISTORY OF the USA is being disputed. For example, the *New York Times* magazine created the 1619 project which "aims to reframe the country's history by placing the consequences of slavery and the contributions of black Americans at the very center of the United States' national narrative."[59] This is more specifically addressed in *The Columbus Initiative* which considers the role of Christians in the abolition of slavery and the settlement of this country. While we recognize the contributions of African Americans in our national heritage, this effort to rewrite our national history through the lens of slavery distorts our past. Addressing the American founding era in greater detail is the project of the next book which details the impact of Christianity in the Renaissance and Reformation on to the Age of Discovery, colonization, and the American Founding Era. For now, let us focus on the present conditions for religion and leadership in our culture.

In the modern United States of America, people seem afraid of being Christian. While there is a courageous and muscular contingent in our churches, many Christians across this country are way too timid. It is written, "Fear not, for I am with you; be not dismayed, for I am your God; I will strengthen you, I will help you, I will uphold you with my righteous right hand" (Isaiah

---

[59] https://www.nytimes.com/interactive/2019/08/14/magazine/1619-america-slavery.html

41:10). Our faith is deep enough to weather any storm, but many Christians give up too quickly. We must not "…shrink from declaring to you the whole counsel of God" (Acts 20:27b). This includes an integrated understanding of the Bible from the Old and New Testaments. This scripture proclaims God's provision and protection in our lives. We are commanded to "Be strong and courageous. Do not be afraid or terrified because of them, for the Lord your God goes with you; he will never leave you nor forsake you" (Joshua 1:6). As we will see, America is a continuation of the urge for freedom. And in the final book in this series, *The Reagan Compromise*, we will see that the reason why America exists was to protect the people of God in the Twentieth Century.

God led the armies of Israel into battle. Jesus is God, and while he is the Lord of the army of hosts, he clearly distinguished between physical and spiritual battles. "I tell you, my friends, do not fear those who kill the body, and after that have nothing more that they can do. But I will warn you whom to fear, fear him who, after he has killed, has authority to cast into hell. Yes, I tell you, fear him!" (Luke 12:4-7). We are to fear God first and foremost, the "fear of the Lord is the beginning of wisdom, and knowledge of the Holy One is understanding" (Proverbs 9:10b). Being fearless is part of the Christian life, "[t]he Lord is my light and my salvation, who should I fear? The Lord is the stronghold of my life, of whom shall I be afraid?" Courage is not the absence of fear but acting despite our fear, or as Franklin D. Roosevelt (1882-1945) said, "Courage is not the absence of fear, but rather the assessment that something else is more important than fear."[60]

---

[60] Kanefield, T. (2019). Franklin D. Roosevelt: The Making of America #5. United States: ABRAMS.

Intimidation of the church may be effective because of the fear that individuals have when confronted with their sin. No one likes being told that they are wicked. A certain portion of the people attending church do not live out a life of faith, instead, they are a part of the church for the sake of the building, children, or socializing rather than devotion to God. Fear in the church may stem from the fact that all Christians are imperfect, and the most devout Christians are grouped with many people who have misrepresented the Christian faith. Hypocrisy is a criticism that does not land upon a person without standards, if you are willing to do anything then nothing is out of bounds. But it can be a devastating critique of a religion that is predicated upon the rejection of Pharisaical legalism. Jesus admonished religious leaders of his day, "Woe to you, scribes and Pharisees, hypocrites! For you tithe mint and dill and cumin and have neglected the weightier matters of the law: justice and mercy and faithfulness. These you ought to have done, without neglecting the others" (Matthew 23:23). However, the standard for the Christian is faithfulness and repentance before God alone and not perfection. Until we embrace the fact all Christians are saints because we are all sinners who are forgiven, we will not be free to act without fear.

The Church Universal

We divide the universal church when we create legalistic factions. The universal church is the Big "C" Church or little "c" catholic body. It is a group of believers across time and space who are unified with Christ as their Lord and Savior. Denominations have served a purpose and the labels we assign to churches or theology makes useful distinctions in terms of the style of worship and teaching. However, the only lines drawn in the

Bible are between light and darkness. "But you are a chosen race, a royal priesthood, a holy nation, a people for his possession, that you may proclaim the excellencies of him who called you out of darkness into his marvelous light" (1 Peter 2:9). We create animosity when hatred of this sinful world is not matched with efforts to reach lost sinners and reconcile nonbelievers to God. Instead in many cases we simply point fingers at sinners rather than inviting them into our churches. We must orient our efforts toward defending the church, hating sin, and unifying under the banner of Christ but too often we fight amongst ourselves.

Some of these fights were important to have when it comes to legitimate debates on doctrinal issues. But, contending these battles at a time when we should agree about more than we disagree does not advance the positive influence of the church in this desperate world. A powerful motto the church once celebrated was, "In essentials unity, in inessentials liberty, in all things charity."[61] But now we accuse others who may be genuinely mistaken as false teachers while we refuse to uniformly call out the worst examples of false teachers who spread lies. How we handle our differences and the way we interpret the Bible are expressions of our faith. Jesus said "A new command I give you: Love one another. As I have loved you, so you must love one another. By this everyone will know that you are my disciples, if you love one another" (John 13:34-35). The whole body should be unified, "Instead, speaking the truth in love, we will grow to become in every respect the mature body of him who is the head, that is, Christ" (Ephesians 4:15). Distinctions between these actions will be fleshed out more fully in the pages to follow.

---

[61] Humphreys, Fisher. The Way We Were: How Southern Baptist Theology Has Changed and What It Means to Us All . Smyth & Helwys Publishing, Inc., 2002.

For now, consider this, the Bible was not written for unbelievers but for those who do believe. The entire book from Genesis to Revelation was written to followers of God, and in the case of the New Testament, Christians specifically. The integrated Bible was preserved for the redeemed disciples of Jesus Christ. So, all the stories about sin and failures are warnings to God's people about our weaknesses. This is not a case for some restitution of a fully catholic and universal church by the efforts of ecumenical human beings. Instead, God will restore the fullness of his church in his time. "For in one Spirit we were all baptized into one body—Jews or Greeks, slaves or free—and all were made to drink of one Spirit" (1 Corinthians 12:13). However, to the extent that believers can, we should agree on certain fundamental truths. God in his infinite wisdom saw fit to reveal Himself to mankind through the fragile and feeble hands of men guided by the Holy Spirit as they wrote His inspired word and passed it down through the centuries.[62] Our understanding of religious practices such as prayer is formed by our doctrine and theology which should be based on the Bible.

The Necessity of Public Faith

Throughout American history, the role of the church in public life has been prominent but ebbing and waning. The founding of the country was based on biblical principles. In 1775, the first Continental Congress opened with a call to prayer. Abraham Lincoln repeatedly beckoned the nation to pray during the Civil War beginning in 1860.[63] In 1952, Harry S. Truman established

---

[62] Geisler, N. L., & Roach, W. C. (2012). Defending inerrancy: Affirming the accuracy of Scripture for a new generation. Baker Books.

[63] Lincoln, A., & Brooks, N. (1990). Second inaugural address (pp. 686-87). Petrarch Press.

the National Day of Prayer to be held on the first Thursday of May.[64] These events and days are our national remembrance stones. Like the way that stones helped the Israelites, "so these stones shall be to the people of Israel a memorial forever" (Joshua 4:7b), days of prayer are established to carry us forward based on our grateful reliance on God. Our holidays like ancient rituals are Holy Days which stand as landmarks in time to pace our years and identify seasons for change.

Prayer is simply the practice of communicating with God, both speaking with Him and listening to Him as he moves our hearts and mind through the Holy Spirit. Our thoughts are oriented toward God in prayer. Our petitions rise to a compassionate and longsuffering Lord who wants to meet our needs with his goodness and mercy. Recent research on mindfulness, meditation, and contemplative practices all affirms the stress-reducing and clarity-inducing role that prayer plays in the life of the believer.[65] The fact that secular therapists and psychologists can research the use of nonreligious breathing exercises, yoga, or Buddhist mantras to achieve similar effects shows that these are only the doorstep of the religious experience. Memorizing many truths of scripture provides spiritual nourishment in an uncertain world. Blessed is the man "whose delight is in the law of the Lord, and who meditates on his law, day and night" (Psalm 1:2). A deep spiritual connection with God starts in peace that "passes all understanding" (Philippians 4:7b), but moves beyond this initial calm. Eventually, prayer grows to inform and drive

---

[64] Fox, F. (1972). The national day of prayer. Theology Today, 29(3), 258-280.
[65] Davis, D. M., & Hayes, J. A. (2011). What are the benefits of mindfulness? A practice review of psychotherapy-related research. Psychotherapy, 48(2), 198.

our sense of purpose. Prayer is the heartbeat of the Christian body pulsing Christ's forgiving blood through our life.

Seeking Truth

The history of Western Civilization is filled with men and women of prayer and study who exhibited leadership through influence. These patriots recognized our need for God's protection and provision, repented of sins, and sought God's face in debates as well as wars. But, from a common source of truth has come many interpretations of this religious system. Therefore, disputes have arisen regarding the proper interpretation of the Bible. In many cases, these are not mere opinions but arguments for or against doctrine and theology which have powerful ramifications for our church and public policy in our nation. Truth corresponds to a collection of propositional facts which may be seen as aggregated into reality.[66] According to Alvin Plantinga, how we understand and interpret scripture will have a direct bearing on our ability to seek truth and make accurate decisions.[67] As the church has grown, discerning the meaning of the Bible has been increasingly important.

Hermeneutics is the study of the interpretation of historical and philosophical texts, especially the Bible. We first interpret the Bible through other biblical passages. The clearest ideas in scripture will inform a proper hermeneutic when dealing with more complex ideas. The revelation of God's plan and intent in the Bible is progressive, meaning that in the Old Testament certain truths are built upon and revealed more fully in the New Testament. There are many foreshadowing references to Jesus

---

[66] Russell, B. (1906, January). On the nature of truth. In Proceedings of the Aristotelian Society (Vol. 7, pp. 28-49). Aristotelian Society, Wiley.
[67] David, M. (2002). The correspondence theory of truth.

in the Jewish Torah.[68] Three verses alone specifically address the coming Messiah, who will be born of a virgin and whose birth we celebrate on Christmas (Genesis 3:15, Micah 5:2, Isaiah 7:14). It is apparent that "The Old Testament proclaims God's mighty acts of redemption. These acts reach a climax in the New Testament when God sends his Son. Redemptive history is the mighty river that runs from the old covenant to the new and holds the two together."[69]

Hermeneutics address the semiotics, semantics, syntax, and presuppositions of language and interpretation.[70] Semiotics is the study of symbols and signs that offer sense-making and meaning-making. Semantics is the study of the meaning of interpretations, the reference points, or propositions for truth. Syntax is a branch of linguistics describing rules, principles, and processes that structure sentences. Presuppositions are the basis for each of these areas, underlying assumptions that are tacitly assumed as premises in an argument or course of action as you interpret a text.

A sound biblical hermeneutic will lead to the proper exegesis of scripture. Exegesis addresses the drawing out of meaning from scripture when dealing with grammar and context. A proper hermeneutic allows us to exegete the text. Using the "grammatical-historical method" you can address the adequacy, consistency, and coherence of your interpretation vis a vie other proposed understandings of any section of scripture. Does your interpretation make sense in light of your understanding of

---

[68] David Limbaugh (2015). Finding Jesus in the Old Testament.

[69] Greidanus, S. (1999). Preaching Christ from the Old Testament: A contemporary hermeneutical method. Wm. B. Eerdmans Publishing.

[70] Ricoeur, P. (1981). Hermeneutics and the human sciences : essays on language, action, and interpretation. Kiribati: Cambridge University Press.

other passages, or are there logical flaws in your position? This is the preferred method for communicating orthodoxy because it affirms that words have meanings and there are facts in history. Both truths are denied by the critical deconstructive schools of literature. Also, through the "redemptive-historical method" we can see the way that God's plan is wrought throughout scripture. There is value in seeing how God has established his plan with the specific aim of reconciling man to himself. This is the goal of creation, to make worshipers of God (see: John 4:23). Both methods help anyone who reads scripture better understand the truths contained therein.

America has suffered many heated arguments about how we should interpret scripture and then how we should act based on our understanding. It is our striving to understand the Bible and God's will that has led to many debates and divisions in the church. Luke commends the Bereans who "received the message with great eagerness and examined the Scriptures every day to see if what Paul said was true" (Acts 17:11b). The result of this pursuit is a higher faithfulness to the truths in scripture. Paul wrote, "I appeal to you, brothers, by the name of our Lord Jesus Christ, that all of you agree, and that there be no divisions among you, but that you be united in the same mind and the same judgment" (1 Corinthians 1:10).

He did not say this so that everyone would get along, quite the contrary. Paul knew that people would disagree and that removing those people who spread falsehoods and lies in an argumentative manner would be required. He told his pupil, "If anyone teaches a different doctrine and does not agree with the sound words of our Lord Jesus Christ and the teaching that accords with godliness, he is puffed up with conceit and understands nothing. He has an unhealthy craving for controversy and for quarrels about words, which produce envy, dissension, slander, evil suspicions, and constant friction among people who are depraved in mind and deprived of the truth, imagining that godliness is a means of gain" (1 Timothy 6:3-5). The problem is not disagreements per se, but those who persist in making trouble either with heresy or an overemphasis on lesser things. Paul admonished the church, "Be careful, however, that the exercise of your rights does not become a stumbling block to the weak" (1 Corinthians 8:9). We should not demand our rights when doing so harms the body of Christ, that is His Church. But we must demand fealty to our Lord and the proper reading of His Word.

We had to work out our differences on many fronts in terms of religious and social questions. These agreements may be one of the greatest miracles that took place in Philadelphia during the 1780s. The American Revolution established states from colonies to uphold and protect individual God-given rights and personal responsibilities of self-government. The Articles of Confederation failed to integrate these disparate jurisdictions into a governable whole. Therefore, the Constitution was needed to create a federal nation-state which allowed and even required that local control at the town, city, county, and state levels be retained.

This structural division of power takes its shape from biblical examples, "For the Lord is our judge, the Lord is our lawgiver, the Lord is our king; it is he who will save us" (Isaiah 33:22). We asserted that there is no King but Jesus, and "the power of the ruler is delegated by the people and continues only with their consent."[71] The gospel was spread throughout the world during

---

[71] George Sabine (1937) A History of Political Theory, Holt, Rinehart and Winston

the Twentieth Century because of the freedom of America. During the American Revolution, patriots rejected the Divine Right of Kings and Thomas Paine (1737-1809) argued that like Israel our "proper Sovereign, the King of Heaven"[72] reigns, echoing Henry Haggar (n.d.), a Leveler, a democratic egalitarian, during the English Civil War,[73] who wrote the pamphlet *No King But Jesus* (1652).[74] All earthly power descends from heavenly authority. This means that in our daily tasks, including those whose work is in government, we should lead according to a proper understanding of God and scripture.

God is the ultimate judge, and, in the end, justice will prevail. In the meantime, we exercise earthly judgment based on our conscience on matters of right and wrong, and we will be held accountable for our actions. God has given us his moral law in the Ten Commandments and laws that uphold these principles align with natural law. Legislators can and should write laws that abide by biblical moral principles because all legislation contains statements on morality. Therefore, any alternative approach to law will promote an alternative form of morality or may even encourage immoral behavior. While we elect presidents, these are mere shadows of the righteous king to come. We rely on human beings to carry out the mantle of leadership without substituting their position for the worship and honor due only to God.

---

[72] Thomas Paine, Common Sense (Girard, Kansas: Haldeman-Julius Co., 1923), 7.

[73] The English Levellers. (1998). United Kingdom: Cambridge University Press.

[74] Haggar, H. (1652). No King But Jesus, or The Walls of Tyrannie Razed. London: Giles Calvert. In Onuf, Peter S. and Thompson, Peter. (2013). In State and Citizen: British America and the Early United States. United Kingdom: University of Virginia Press.

Leaders are accountable to the people, "And Moses came and told the people all the words of the Lord, and all the judgments: and all the people answered with one voice, and said, All the words which the Lord has said will we do" (Exodus 24:3). The Constitutional provisions for the Congress in a House of Representatives and Senate mirror British systems which draw from Old Testament, Greek, and Roman polity. We select our leaders and judges, "Then the Lord said to Moses, 'Gather for me seventy men of the elders of Israel, whom you know to be the elders of the people and officers over them'" (Numbers 11:16). The idea of a council of elders is common across cultures and religions, however, the American system uniquely draws from this Judeo-Christian heritage. Lawmakers, rulers, and judges must be elected by the communities they represent, "Choose for your tribes wise, understanding, and experienced men, and I will appoint them as your heads" (Deuteronomy 1:13). Congress, in our Republic, is a form of participative leadership in which representatives of the people speak out on issues and write laws.[75] This reflects the ethical aspects of leadership where "leadership is not a person or a position. It is a complex moral relationship between people, based on trust, obligation, commitment, emotion, and a shared vision of the good."[76]

Pushing accountability to the lowest possible level and decentralizing decision-making allows for states to act as experiments in democracy and have control over a majority of the immediate and personal decisions individuals face.[77] The American

---

[75] Tannenbaum, R., & Schmidt, W. H. (2009). How to choose a leadership pattern. Harvard Business Review Press.

[76] Ciulla, J. B. (2003). The ethics of leadership. Wadsworth/Thomson Learning.

[77] Fukuyama, F. (2014). States and democracy. Democratization, 21(7), 1326-1340.

Civil War provided the starkest example of the consequences of our quarrels. This existential crisis for our country is explored in *The Lincoln Legacy*. Principles for the division and delegation of power remain a source of controversy. Jurisdictional disputes may arise when the people accede to laws at higher levels. Through authoritarian power grabs at the federal level or the danger of petty tyrants in localities, natural law is subverted. The federal, state, and city responses to the COVID-19 pandemic, in 2020, exemplify these problems across the world.[78] Different countries have implemented varied policies, but the effectiveness of these policies has not been studied. Each city, state, and country must be examined to determine which policies have proven most successful in reducing the threat of this virus to citizens. This is a recent and salient example of the way that government power is used poorly. It highlights the challenges of using federal power to implement a one-size-fits-all policy in a situation that demands empirical adjustments.

It is important to place this conversation about politics in the proper context. A more unified and engaged role for the Christian church based on our laws and history in the United States is needed. We have a right and duty to persevere in the face of opposition when it comes to maintaining our nation's character and morality. We must stand against the secularization of our institutions which we specifically designed to allow people of any faith or no faith at all the ability to participate in our national discourse. These actions preserve and protect freedom for all citizens because without these values implicit in the Christian faith a vacuum will ensue to be filled by more

---

[78] Moisio, S. (2020). State power and the COVID-19 pandemic: the case of Finland. Eurasian Geography and Economics, 1-8.

totalitarian ideologies. Taking advantage of these allowances many groups have pushed the right and proper expressions of faith into a corner. These intimidation tactics must end.

4

The March of History

AS CHRISTIANITY CONTINUES to spread across the world it no longer occupies the position of prominence in US legal or political life.[79] Christians are 31.2 percent of the world population according to the Pew Research Center, greatly exceeding Islam especially if forced conversion and cultural attachments are controlled for in studies and corrected.[80] Religion, as we will see, must be a choice. It is not something you can be born with or into. The reason for the decline in the American church is because Christians have too often refrained from participating in the public square and allowed a vacuum of ideology to exist. Nature abhors a vacuum and the same is true in societies. In many cases, Christians who hold office do so for their benefit and may pay lip service to a civic religion rather than fidelity to the one true God. We cannot be lukewarm milquetoast believers and expect to have the full impact of salt and light (see: Matthew 5:13-16). This vacuum has been filled by various pseudo-religious systems from Marxism, secularism, feminism, environmentalism, to identity politics.

History informs the present. And, our current actions as a people are linked to our past. Therefore, as we plumb the depths

---

[79] Kim, S., & Kim, K. (2016). Christianity as a world religion: An introduction. Bloomsbury Publishing.
[80] Hackett, C., & McClendon, D. (2017). Christians remain world's largest religious group, but they are declining in Europe. Pew Research Center.

of our national story and draw from our archives we can gain guidance and perspective for decision-making today.

This generation of leaders will determine if Christianity continues to play a prominent role in our nation's future. The case of *Greece v. Galloway* is but one example of the legal battles about religion in our country. According to William Stuntz (1958-2011): "In America's legal conversation, Christianity is an unwelcome guest."[81] He rejects this ostracization of faith in our courts and government and supports Christian legal scholars who craft a Christian legal theory that is specifically tied to our heritage, in political and social movements such as Civil Rights and Pro-life. Numerous groups have been formed for the express purpose of instilling and defending Christian policies and positions in government and law. Many of these organizations specifically provide advocacy for Christians. The Christian Legal Society is "dedicated to serving Jesus Christ through the practice and study of law, the defense of religious freedom and life, and the provision of legal aid to the needy."[82]

In terms of religious freedom, two recently decided cases show that conservative justices are upholding the Constitution and even liberals on the court can find common ground in terms of our first amendment protections. In 2019, in the case *Our Lady of Guadalupe School v. Morrisey-Berru*, the US Supreme Court found 7-2 that civil courts may not adjudicate anti-religious discrimination claims against private religious schools. During the same term, in *Little Sisters of the Poor Saints Peter and Paul Home v. Pennsylvania*, the court found that the Trump administration could provide religious and conscientious objection

---

[81] Stuntz, W., McConnel, Cochran, R. & Carmella (2003). Christian Legal Theory. Harvard Law Review, 116(6), 1707-1749.
[82] https://www.christianlegalsociety.org/

exemptions to Obamacare. And, in 2020, the Supreme Court in *Espinoza v. Montana Department of Revenue* ruled that states could not prohibit religious schools from receiving scholarship money under tax-credit programs. At best we are gaining ground lost but this is needed. The fact that Christian schools and charities must fight for equal treatment demonstrates that religion is under legal assault. Throughout the last fifty years, hundreds of religious cases have been argued at various levels of the US judicial system.[83] But, if our right to worship God hinges on the rulings of nine people in black robes, we have no freedom.[84]

Legal Persecution

The Alliance Defending Freedom (ADF), founded in 1994, is a legal advocacy organization supporting religious liberty, human life, freedom of speech, marriage, and family.[85] The ADF has clear guiding principles, claiming that the United States legal system was built on a Christian foundation. It is based on the belief that the clearest interpretation of morality and law proceeds from the Christian religious and biblical worldview. With more than 3,100 attorneys and $223 million plus worth of legal billable hours donated the ADF has won nearly 80 percent of its cases. It has played a part in fifty-six victories at the Supreme Court of the United States level.[86] This is a key part of the fight we must embrace. Christians are not persecuted when we go along with the demands of an unjust system. Only when we reject unjust laws will we suffer for Christ, "Then they left the

---

[83] https://www.adflegal.org/
[84] Levin, M. R. (2006). Men in Black: How the Supreme Court Is Destroying America. United States: Regnery Publishing.
[85] ibid
[86] https://aclj.org/

presence of the council, rejoicing that they were counted worthy to suffer dishonor for the name" (Acts 5:41).

The American Center for Law & Justice (ACLJ) is a Christian legal advocacy organization in Washington, D.C. Founded in 1990 by Pat Robertson (b. 1930) the Chancellor of Regent University, Chairman of *The Christian Broadcasting Network* (CBN), and a prominent televangelist, the ACLJ has been on the forefront of the battle between the church and culture. Robertson received his J.D. from Yale law school, never passed the bar exam, or practiced as an attorney however maintained an interest in law. The organization is associated with Regent University School of Law in Virginia Beach, VA. The chief counsel is Jay Sekulow (b. 1956), a lawyer, radio host, and was the lead outside counsel to Donald Trump in his 2020 impeachment trial.

The ACLJ has argued for First Amendment rights of abortion protesters (ex. *Operation Rescue v. National Organization for Women*, 2006), establishment clause cases (ex. *Board of Education of the Westside Community Schools v. Mergens*, 1990, and *Locke v. Davey*, 2004), and "equal access" of religious groups to public resources.[87] The ACLJ has internationally expanded its strategy to fight legal battles on behalf of Christians through the European Centre for Law and Justice (ECLJ) in Strasbourg, Germany, the Slavic Centre for Law and Justice (SCLJ), and The African Centre for Law and Justice (ACLJ). It has also funded a project called Be Heard to "demand that world governments respect the most basic human rights and human dignity of persecuted believers."[88]

---

[87] ibid
[88] https://beheardproject.com/

To defend the gospel of Jesus Christ many Christians have taken legal actions including filing cases that are meant to carve out religious protections we took for granted. Now Christians ask: How should we deal with these challenges to our faith and freedom? How far do we press our rights and seek justice? We must continually relitigate each false accusation used to dispirit us. To avoid these attacks many Christians have felt the need to retreat and pull back. The desire for self-protection and survival is natural but avoiding a needed conflict may invite more aggression. In many cases, the proper resolution of differences is necessary to advance our cause. Occasionally we must stand our ground and fight for ourselves, our family, and our nation. "If possible, so far as it depends on you, live peaceably with all" (Romans 12:18).

Some believers, such as Rod Dreher (b. 1967), essentially suggest that we cede the ground to secularists and retreat from engaging in culture and politics.[89] He contended that Christians now must deal with the fact this is no longer a Christian culture, which is explored in *The Reagan Compromise*. He recommends that we ought to pull back as much as we can and become hermits. We should stay in our holy huddle and develop private Christian groups, communes if you will. Saint Benedict of Nursia (c. 480-547) established twelve cloisters of monks.[90] Dreher takes inspiration from these vaults of learning and human advancement which protected the faith during the brutality in the Middle Ages that followed the breakdown of the Roman Empire. But his solution is woefully inadequate to the threats we face. It was the

---

[89] Dreher, R. (2017). The Benedict option: a strategy for Christians in a post-Christian nation. Penguin.
[90] The Rule of St. Benedict in English. (2016). United States: Liturgical Press.

Christian church that transformed a pagan culture and empire into a multiethnic truth-seeking people.[91]

Instead of hiding, Christians should boldly participate in our federal, state, and local governments.[92] We have a moral obligation to do so. We have done so throughout history and the results speak for themselves. The challenges and successes of Christianity are included in our defense of freedom alongside the advance scientific knowledge, technology, health, and peace. Mischaracterizing our goals and actions as White Christian Nationalism or dominionism theocracy is slander (oral) and libel (written) against Christians, the church, and Jesus. A more biblical approach to governance is seen as a threat by people who are afraid of the significant influence that morality and religion have on our population. Why would these individuals want to avoid the universal and deep truths of scripture which have so profoundly changed our world for the better? One may only speculate, but in many cases rejecting Jesus stems from a refusal to submit to the lordship of an eternal and omnipotent God.

Christian Reconstruction

One of the most maligned Christian thinkers by the left in the Twentieth Century is Rousas Jonas Rushdoony (1916-2001). Rushdoony used the term Reconstruction to describe his vision of a comprehensive philosophy or worldview that made the whole Bible the source and measure of all life. Jeff Sharlet (b. 1972), writing in *Harper's Magazine* about the surprising resilience of

---

[91] Russell, J. B. (1968). Medieval Civilization. United States: Wipf & Stock Publishers.
[92] McVicar, M. J. (2015). Christian Reconstruction: R. J. Rushdoony and American Religious Conservatism. United States: University of North Carolina Press.

"the dupes, the saps, and the fools—the believers", believes that "The Christian nation of which the movement dreams, a government of those chosen by God but democratically elected by a people who freely accept His will as their own, is a far country." [93] His critique of Christian Reconstruction is simply an anti-religious screed. He attempts to dispel the notion that Christians played a central part in the United States' founding and have any right to assert their role in deciding the future of this country. This instinct by some people to rewrite history and propagandize secularism is a topic that must be returned to repeatedly.

Consider the role in our government of the Church that has always sought greater involvement in people's lives. Impacting public policy is but one expression of our desire to redeem the culture around us. Rushdoony offers some accurate critiques and logical arguments about the direction of our society, but his political positions are impractical in this present day and age. A generalized version of Christian nationalism propounds these distinctions between dominion theology, American populism, and conservative politics. We will explore the ways that Christians can and should be more patriotic and nationalistic while maintaining the highest loyalty to God alone.

More broadly, a sociological approach to understanding the influence of religion in public life has yielded surprisingly little insight into the role Christianity can and should play in our nation. Instead, authors such as Sara Diamond, an attorney, and sociologist who received her undergraduate degree from UC Irvine, Ph.D. from UC Berkeley in Sociology, and J.D. from the UC Hastings College of Law, warn Americans about the threat

---

[93] Sharlet, J. (2006). Through A Glass, Darkly How the Christian right is reimagining US history. Harpers, 1879, 33.

from a burgeoning theocracy. She is a prototype of the California system of higher education. She has written four books about the Christian right, asserting that "the primary importance of the ideology is its role as a catalyst for what is loosely called 'dominion theology.'"[94] She coined the term "dominionism" to describe conservative Christians using the most ardent brand of theology to paint a large proportion of this country with a broad brush.

Diamond's analysis concludes that "the concept that Christians are biblically mandated to 'occupy' all secular institutions has become the central unifying ideology for the Christian Right." Note the military language used. Christians make distinctions between physical and spiritual warfare. Every position, policy, and project in government is a form of taking over this country, the only question is what agenda and worldview will be promoted. Distinctions between Christian activism may bleed into one another if we do not do a good job distinguishing between the type of effort we apply in different spheres. This is an essential aspect of Abraham Kuyper's (1837-1920) description of sphere sovereignty.[95] Diamond extends the perspective of a minority position held by a few radical Christians to all conservatives. This is typical of liberalism, labeling Christian positions as reactionary to silence opposition. She thinks that Christians are attempting to take over this nation as if the church did not play an integral role in the founding of this nation and will not be essential to its future. Many traditional Christians are simply trying to maintain what is good, true, and beautiful.

---

[94] Diamond, S. (1990). Spiritual warfare: The politics of the Christian right (Vol. 144). Black Rose Books Ltd.
[95] Kuyper, A. (2015). Our Program: A Christian Political Manifesto. United States: Faithlife Corporation.

Diamond gives voice to concerns about the mobilization of conservative power and influence in the government that many leftists share. As an overt and outspoken liberal, she is concerned about the way that the Christian church is controlling the Republican party. She recommends Communist revolutions to destroy capitalism and commends the USSR for leading anti-colonial national liberation movements.[96] But she is crippled by the fear of a church that preaches the "truth in love" (Ephesians 4:15). The Bush family dynasty, according to Diamond, were evangelical Christians taking over this nation. Set aside the religious practice of one family, this notion of a takeover is patently absurd. Christians have played a necessary role in the function of this country since its inception. Any attempt to rewrite history and downplay the role of faith in our nation is deceptive. Dispelling this method of historical revisionism alone does not fully capture the raw hatred of religion that Diamond and others like her have.

Political Alliances

Deconstructing conservatism into a blend of anticommunists, evangelicals, and neoconservatives implies that disparate interests overlap rather than emanating from a common root. The reasons why Christians oppose tyranny is explored further in *The Columbus Initiative*. Secularists attack the church because religion is linked to public policy. Rather than addressing the shortcomings of Socialism and Communism, the left uses a common slur, White (read: of European descent) conservative Christians are the racist, sexist, homophobic, xenophobic

---

[96] Mohamed Salih, M. A. (2007). African liberation movement governments and democracy. Democratization, 14(4), 669-685.

bigots.[97] For socialists, there is no debate with Christians who are seen as evil, even though Christians preach a gospel of self-sacrifice, love, and forgiveness. "Woe to those who call evil good and good evil, who put darkness for light and light for darkness, who put bitter for sweet and sweet for bitter" (Isaiah 5:20). The three-legged stool of Reagan Republicanism which defined the Grand Old Party (GOP) for a generation reflects what the left opposes policy-wise. The Republican party supports social, economic, and national security positions that align with biblical, traditional, and constitutional principles. Falsely attaching to the Republican Party white supremacists and anti-segregation views encourage attacks on Christians designed to silence intellectual dissent.

When it comes to the acts of governance, laws, executive orders, court rulings, and agency mandates often reflect the pull of power and money on leaders. Our laws are shaped by many forces other than ethical legal reasoning. Politics in the United States has been greatly influenced by lobbyists and intellectual policy wonks. An example of the latter is the Ripon Society. A Republican think tank founded in 1962 their mission is to "promote the ideas and principles that have made America great and contributed to the GOP's success."[98] Their purpose is to research intermediating institutions such as religious groups that serve the community through faith-based initiatives.[99] However, because of the ongoing efforts of liberals during the twentieth century, these community-minded groups have been gutted. Welfare has supplanted religious aid and individual charity.

---

[97] https://www.axios.com/bernie-sanders-donald-trump-racist-sexist-homophobic-6da0fbe8-695a-492d-883d-865fdb96af6c.html
[98] https://riponsociety.org/the-ripon-society-mission/
[99] https://www.catholicculture.org/commentary/intermediary-institutions-represent-preserve-and-shape-robust-culture/

Since World War II, civic organizations have attempted to replace the need for churches such as John F. Kennedy's (1917-1963) Peace Corps (1961), George H.W. Bush's (1924-2018) Thousand Points of Light Foundation (1990), and Bill Clinton's (b. 1946) AmeriCorps (1993). George W. Bush's (b. 1946) faith-based initiative was meant to partner with churches and religious charities to push back on secularizing federal requirements. Unfortunately, many churches became co-opted by government oversight. As the Supreme Court shifted from strict separationism to "equal treatment", churches were replaced with programs such as the Charitable Choice principles enacted by President Clinton. The George W. Bush administration began the Ready4Work (employment assistance for ex-prisoners), the Access to Recovery program (substance abuse), and the PEPFAR program (fighting AIDS in Africa) all funneling federal dollars through non-profit and faith-based organizations such as African-American churches to help individuals in need. Federal programs must support the religious protections in the 1964 Civil Rights Act. But, federal money may not benefit individuals and instead often corrupt these causes. We should look no further than the ongoing threat to remove the tax-exempt status of certain churches to see who is pulling the strings.

Government interaction with the church is a crucially important aspect of our national and civic life. Church leaders have dealt with this issue since the beginning of Christianity. Even Jesus deftly avoided being called a zealot and told his disciples, "Therefore render to Caesar the things that are Caesar's, and to God the things that are God's" (Matthew 22:2). Much ink has been split on the theme of the relationship between church and state. The church needs to foster a proper understanding of its authority and responsibility within spheres of sovereignty. Family, church, community, economy, society, and government should occupy separate areas of power and influence. This is where we turn to a significant historical marker, Constantine the Great (272-337).

Constantinople

Constantine became emperor of Rome, in 306, well after Pax Romana and about 100 years before the fall of the Roman Empire. He is a compelling historical character because many people are familiar with his name but do not know his story or why he matters to American history. His efforts to expand and protect the church led to America's eventual rise as a nation after 1400 years of increasing freedom, science, and wisdom. Christianity has a common history that all believers share, with roots back through the Middle Ages and Rome to Jerusalem. Jesus' resurrection set off a chain of events that will culminate in his second coming. We are meant to expand the church, "For the earth will be filled with the knowledge of the glory of the Lord as the waters cover the sea" (Habakkuk 2:14). In the meantime, the church has taken on the evangelical mission to share His gospel with all people.

Often the story of America is conflated with that of Western Civilization, and we certainly draw from this rich tapestry of ideas. However, it was not Judaism, Greek philosophy, or Roman law that most animated the American Revolution. The subsequent legal system has been built on the pillars of faith and practice that guide the Christian Church. When you compare the differences between the trajectory of European and American versions of democracy you find that in the USA mobs and elitism had been tempered by a religious streak that is presently being stamped out. It was Christian governance, which began in the reign of

Constantine, that expanded a fledgling religion, allowing it to spread across the globe sowing freedom in its wake. God's plan is written in the lives of men and women and in hindsight we see His providence in his selection of Constantine and many events that followed. We would not be here today if it were not for men and women of faith who led, fought, and died for the cause of Christ.

When I attended a conference in Istanbul, the capital of Constantine's Eastern Empire, I spent time at the Hagia Sophia, and the Sultan Ahmet grounds. This beautiful city is the intersection of culture and religion as Asia meets Europe and remains an important hinge of history. It's known throughout the world as an ancient city that has withstood numerous sieges. You may be familiar with the lyrics from the song "Istanbul (Not Constantinople)" by The Four Lads, "Istanbul was Constantinople, now it's Istanbul, not Constantinople. Been a long time gone, Constantinople, now it's Turkish delight on a moonlit night." As a City on Seven Hills, like Rome, it also continues to impact this world.

This city, forged in blood, has a unique history that leads us to examine Constantine more closely. It was originally a strategic port city, Byzantium, which became an outpost dedicated to the preservation of the Christian church. Asia Minor which is now Turkey was peppered with churches during the early era of Christian history. Now the Hagia Sophia, which was built in 537 as a cathedral in the Roman Empire and served the Greek Eastern Orthodox Church then became a museum was recently converted into a mosque.[100] The Parliamentary Assembly of the

---

[100] Nelson, R. S. (2004). Hagia Sophia, 1850-1950: holy wisdom modern monument. University of Chicago Press.

Council of Europe's Culture Committee condemned the move initiated by the bold and aggressive Turkish Sunni Islamic president Recep Tayyip Erdoğan (b. 1954). This effort is part of the Neo-Ottoman policy that uses Islam as a foil against the West and stirs anti-Western sentiment in Turkey.[101] Religion remains a source of great controversy, passion, and fervor in our world. It is a part of who we are.

Analyzing our history through the lens of religion and leadership makes it clearer how Christianity helps us lead a life pleasing to the Lord. This includes the way we raise our family and serve our country. Faith encourages us to do our jobs well, and that includes the job of governing. "Whatever you do, work heartily, as for the Lord and not for men" (Colossians 3:23). We need more men and women who see their lives as an extension of their faith. The interaction between religion and society in the UAE provides another lesson. In the emirates talking about religion is not off-limits. Conversations about faith are natural and expected. Religion should not be a taboo subject. In America, being open and honest about your thoughts, convictions, or questions on the topic of religion is considered worse than swearing. We must recover the proper place of religion in our national discourse to improve moral behavior in a thriving civilization.

---

[101] Langan, M. (2017). Virtuous power Turkey in sub-Saharan Africa: the 'Neo-Ottoman'challenge to the European Union. Third World Quarterly, 38(6), 1399-1414.

5

A God-shaped Hole

BLAISE PASCAL (1623-1662), a French philosopher and Catholic theologian, wrote, "What else does this craving, and this helplessness, proclaim but that there was once in man a true happiness, of which all that now remains is the empty print and trace? This he tries in vain to fill with everything around him, seeking in things that are not there the help he cannot find in those that are, though none can help, since this infinite abyss can be filled only with an infinite and immutable object; in other words, by God himself."[102] This so-called God-shaped hole is found in all humans across all races, times, and places. It is a fact of psychology across cultures that human beings struggle with forms of dissatisfaction and that depression is a modern epidemic.[103] St. Augustine (354-430) wrote, "You have made us for yourself, O Lord, and our hearts are restless until they rest in you."[104] We all need guidance from the transcendent and super-natural to make sense of the amazing cosmos around us. The universe begs for an explanation. The human heart needs some-thing to worship, to orient our lives around a comprehensive and coherent narrative. This is the nature of religion, it engages our reason, stills our passion, and focuses our attention on God,

[102] Pascal, B. (1852). Pensées. Dezobry and Magdeleine.
[103] Ingram, R. E., Miranda, J., & Segal, Z. V. (1998). Cognitive vulnerability to depression (pp. 88-115). New York: Guilford Press.
[104] Augustine, S. (398). St. Augustine's Confessions (Vol. 26). W. Heinemann.

to whom all glory and honor are due. It is the proper posture of man to bow before the Almighty.

It is necessary to define religion in sociological terms to understand how it has affected our history. This is not a history of religion, nor a philosophical treatise on theism. It is a retrospective comparison of Christianity to other religions. This addresses de jure rather than de facto objections to Christianity.[105] Apologetics can also provide a practical defense of mankind's theistic instinct. Christians should "in your hearts honor Christ the Lord as holy, always being prepared to make a defense to anyone who asks you for a reason for the hope that is in you; yet do it with gentleness and respect" (1 Peter 3:15). While many philosophical and theological topics are relevant the thrust of this chapter is the sociological underpinnings of belief. Separate volumes have been written in defense of the truthfulness of the Christian faith. We will explore the basic common assumptions we make as human beings about the transcendent and our place in the universe. Understanding how religion shapes us will explain how we should shape our society, culture, and nation.

Homo Religiosus

Human beings were created in God's image. However, since the fall of man, we have fought against our sin nature and our brothers. To consolidate power and assist our group's survival we banded together in families and tribes. Our nations were built around groups of people who cooperate in collective actions such as hunting and farming. In Genesis, the table of nations outlines the descendants who populated the earth,

---

[105] Plantinga, A. (2000). Warranted Christian belief. United Kingdom: Oxford University Press.

"Now these are the generations of the sons of Noah; Shem, Ham, and Japheth: and unto them were sons born after the flood" (Genesis 10:1). These people searched for meaning amid a world full of threatening and demanding circumstances. The branches of humanity splintered into various forms of religious assumptions, ideas, ceremonies, and practices each expressing aspects or perversions of the original faith. These same groups will be reassembled in heaven, "After this I looked, and there before me was a great multitude that no one could count, from every nation, tribe, people, and language, standing before the throne and before the Lamb. They were wearing white robes and were holding palm branches in their hands" (Revelation 7:9). The instinct to worship God is universal.

We are religious creatures, so anthropology and theology are linked. God made us for Himself, "You made him for a little while lower than the angels; you have crowned him with glory and honor" (Hebrews 2:7). So much of human life is attached to our worship, our contemplation of death, and meaning. The biblical story of creation is the oldest version of this account passed down through generations of oral tradition. Therefore, Christianity can lay claim to the world's oldest religion, even though we do not have Genesis recorded on steles or walls but parchment by the people of Israel.

Religious and philosophical thinkers contemplate the nature of man. Carl Linnaeus (1707-1778), a Swedish botanist and taxonomist (someone who builds categories of terms), coined the phrase homo sapiens to group human beings as "wise men" in terms of our genus and species.[106] Likewise,

---

[106] Spamer, Earle E (29 January 1999). "Know Thyself: Responsible Science and the Lectotype of Homo sapiens Linnaeus, 1758". Proceedings of the Academy of Natural Sciences. 149 (1): 109–14. JSTOR 4065043.

Aristotle (384–322 BC) called man the rational animal.[107] An often-quoted Islamic hadith or teaching, possibly from Qatada ibn Di'ama (d. 735) states, "God created the angels from intellect without sensuality, the beasts from sensuality without intellect, and humanity from both intellect and sensuality. So, when a person's intellect overcomes his sensuality, he is better than the angels, but when his sensuality overcomes his intellect, he is worse than the beasts."[108]

For the Christian, humans are made by God to become more like him, "So God created man in his image, in the image of God he created him; male and female he created them" (Genesis 1:27). Neo-Darwinists have attempted reclamation of the origin of the species in a sociological Darwinism (not Social Darwinism), using evolutionary theory to explain our religious instincts and changes in society. This assumes certain scientific facts about the origin and constitution of mankind but makes broader arguments about how human social processes have grown through memes.[109] A single-couple of human origin is possible according to various models and "allele frequency spectra and linkage disequilibrium statistics from current genetic data."[110] Joshua Swamidass (b. 1978), professor and genomic medicine researcher at Washington University in Saint Louis, has offered a mathematical and genealogical rather than genetic explanation for common descent from a single human pair, Adam and Eve[111]

---

[107] Sosa, E., & Galloway, D. (2000). Man the rational animal?. Synthese, 122(1-2), 165-178.

[108] Nasr, S. H. (1987). Islamic Spirituality: Foundations. Taylor & Francis.

[109] Dawkins, R., & Davis, N. (2017). The selfish gene. Macat Library.

[110] Hössjer, O., & Gauger, A. (2019). A single-couple human origin is possible. BIO-Complexity, 2019.

[111] Swamidass, S. J. (2019). The Genealogical Adam and Eve: The Surprising Science of Universal Ancestry. United Kingdom: InterVarsity Press.

while affirming the population theory of homo sapiens,[112] that primates rose in a group. However similar human and chimpanzee DNA, between 96-99 percent of the information,[113] may be compared to the deeper and more significant correspondence between the molecular properties of rain clouds and watermelon, both are over 90 percent water.

It is that which distinguishes us from other creatures, not the similarities, that matters. Our eternal souls, rational capacity, and creative drive are unique in the created order. If we are in the family tree of animals as multicellular eukaryotic (with a nucleus) organisms that breathe, eat, and reproduce then we are the golden branch fully distinct in many ways from the other creatures in God's creation. Jonathan Haidt (b. 1963) points out that many cultures make distinctions between humans and other animals because of the adaptations in diet and social groups that man has made[114] when he points out that religious instinct and cleanliness stems from the way that "disgust is the guardian of the body."[115] Our efforts at ritual holiness mirror God's essential properties.

The Bible iterates this sacred nature of the human body instead of decrying the corruption of the flesh, "Or do you not know that your body is a temple of the Holy Spirit within you, whom you have from God? You are not your own, for you were

---

[112] Ayala, F. J., Escalante, A., O'Huigin, C., & Klein, J. (1994). Molecular genetics of speciation and human origins. Proceedings of the National Academy of Sciences, 91(15), 6787-6794.
[113] https://www.genome.gov/
[114] Haidt, J., Rozin, P., Mccauley, C., & Imada, S. (1997). Body, Psyche, and Culture: The Relationship between Disgust and Morality. Psychology and Developing Societies, 9(1), 107–131.
[115] Haidt, J. (2012). The righteous mind: Why good people are divided by politics and religion. Vintage.

bought with a price. So, glorify God in your body" (1 Corinthians 6:19-20). Our religious practice reinforces these differences in the way that humans and animals perform basic biological functions such as eating and reproduction. "Yet you have made him a little lower than the heavenly beings and crowned him with glory and honor" (Psalm 8:5). Regardless of the possibility of interbreeding between neanderthal and human ancestors or the mythical-historical qualities of the creation account, the origin of life itself remains a mystery that requires a miraculous explanation.[116]

Are some people uniquely gifted with a sense of the divine? If so, then this gift comes from God and is given according to his will. However, it is too simplistic to elevate some people to the status of religious-minded and leave others in the secular domain. All of mankind aspires to know God. Some scholars attempt to conflate the personal nature of religion with a subjective quality rather than institutional structure. Friedrich Schleiermacher (1768-1834), a German theologian,[117] emphasized religion as an attribute of certain people who recognize their dependence on God.[118] Max Scheler (1874-1928), a German Philosopher wrote: "The man who has God in his heart and God in his actions, who in his spiritual figure is a transformer of souls is religious."[119]

---

[116] Craig, W. L. (2021). In Quest of the Historical Adam: A Biblical and Scientific Exploration. United States: William B. Eerdmans Publishing Company.

[117] Schleiermacher, Friedrich. The Christian Faith, translated by H. R. Mackintosh and J. S. Stewart (1929; reprint, New York, 1963).

[118] Schleiermacher, F. (1991). Friedrich Schleiermacher: Pioneer of modern theology (Vol. 1). Fortress Press.

[119] Max Scheler, On the Eternal in Man, "The Essence of Philosophy and the Moral Preconditions of Philosophical Knowledge" trans. Bernard Noble (New York: Harper & Brothers, 1960)

These authors seem to think that like the Great Man Theory of leadership,[120] some people have been given an abundance of spiritual sensitivity. Joachim Wach (1898-1955)[121] developed his understanding of man's religious nature based on the writing of Max Weber (1864-1920), a German sociologist, and proposed that *homo religiosus* is a sociological phenomenon. Gerardus van der Leeuw (1890-1950), a Dutch historian of religion, contrasted his sociological *homo religiosus* to describe humanity with Scheler's individualist views. Wilhelm Dupré (b. 1936) describes religion as a "universal pattern of human self-realization" and a "constitutive presence ... in the emergence of man."[122] All of these explanations attempt in some way to get around the relationship between mankind and the creator God.

After throwing up his hands in despair, John Caputo (b. 1940), a professor of philosophy at Syracuse University, informs us, "Religion in the singular, as just one thing, is nowhere to be found; it is too maddeningly polyvalent and too uncontainably diverse."[123] Instead, he appeals to religion as a "love of God." However, though this definition points us in the right direction, toward God, it fails to capture the ideological nature of religion. According to Clifford Geertz (1926-2006), an anthropologist, a religion is: (1) a system of symbols that acts to (2) establish powerful, pervasive, and long-lasting moods and motivations in men by (3) formulating conceptions of a general order of existence and (4) clothing these conceptions with such an aura of factuality that (5) the moods and motivations seem uniquely

---

[120] Spector, B. A. (2016). Carlyle, Freud, and the great man theory more fully considered. Leadership, 12(2), 250-260.
[121] Joachim Wach. Sociology of Religion (1944)
[122] Dupré, Wilhelm. Religion in Primitive Cultures: A Study in Ethnophilosophy (Paris, 1975).
[123] Caputo, J. (2018). On religion. Routledge.

realistic.[124] This definition is vaguely psychological which may be relevant to a study of religious experience for individuals but not religion as fact, holistically and sociologically.

Emile Durkheim (1858-1917), a prominent French sociologist, described religion as a collective experience directed toward the sacred.[125] Jonathan Z. Smith (1938-2017) referred to a "sacred persistence" found in religion. Our instinct is toward the sacred in reverence and worship and away from the secular and mundane. That which is sacred has consistently also been viewed as blessed by the deity to be revered and worshiped. This attribute has been associated with the holiness of the Christian God. Mircea Eliade (1907-1986), a Romanian historian, focused on religious experiences in *hierophanies*, the manifestation of the sacred as opposed to our natural, daily, experiences of profane space and time which we call secular life.[126] He pointed to the undeniable religious structures in the modern world.[127] Robert F. Brown (b. 1941) echoes this view when he offers that religion is "the organic and psychological constitution of homo sapiens."[128] Seeking God is part of who and what we are.

The Stanford Philosophical Dictionary, a reliable source of secular knowledge, after begging off, offers this definition: "Religion involves a communal, transmittable body of teachings and prescribed practices about an ultimate, sacred reality

---

[124] Banton, M., Geertz, C. (1966). Religion as a Cultural System. United Kingdom: Tavistock.

[125] Durkheim, É. (1912). Les formes élémentaires de la vie religieuse: le système totémique en Australie (Vol. 4). Alcan.

[126] Eliade, M. (2013). The quest: History and meaning in religion. University of Chicago Press.

[127] Eliade. The Sacred and the Profane (New York, 1959)

[128] Robert F. Brown's "Eliade on Archaic Religion: Some Old and New Criticisms," Studies in Religion / Sciences religieuses 10 (1981)

or state of being...”[129] This definition rightly acknowledges the sacred aspect of religion but goes on to expand a theoretical definition in terms of various practices which waters it down. Most of these definitions fail to capture the fundamental nature of religion as a worldview, or lens through which humans understand and interpret reality.

Religion mediates the relationship between the sacred and secular and points us toward God. Worldviews include secular ideologies which take on religious overtones as a substitute for the meaning-making engine in people's lives that removes God from the equation. In the book *Flatland*, a fictional story about shapes experiencing new realities when a two-dimensional object "sees" three dimensions it cannot explain what it means to be elevated, this describes secular thinking that denies the higher plane of spiritual life and thus cannot explain the transcendent.[130] Each version of religion responds to the question of theism: who is God? This is a simplified view of religion that allows us to explore its varied aspects.

Theism is the simple claim that God exists.[131] While this belief is independent of cultural trappings, belief in God generally stems from creation mythology about God as the originator and initiator of the universe. Humans tend to seek God, at a basic level, as the answer to the origin of our shared experience in common existence. Stories have been written to circumscribe truths of pre-history in a narrative. Secularism, on the other hand, is the belief that this world, our history, and the physical reality in this present age, are all that exists and matters. Humans

---

[129] https://plato.stanford.edu/entries/philosophy-religion/
[130] Abbott, E. (2009). Flatland. Broadview Press.
[131] Mackie, J. L., & MacKie, J. L. (1982). The Miracle of Theism: Arguments for and against the Existence of God (p. 15). Oxford: Clarendon Press.

take on a "buffered identity" where they are not influenced by religion and live in a disenchanted world in which supernatural beings are nearly impossible.[132] Secularism is a form of materialism often woven with philosophical assumptions about mankind and history.

Monotheism is the belief that there is only one single God. This is the most exclusive form of religion because it rejects the allure of polytheism which attempts to placate many gods, spreading sacrifices and loyalty around. Much of the early forms of religion were polytheistic. Polytheism is a belief in a multiplicity of gods, small "g" gods are in a panoply of earthly deities. They often took on human-like forms and shared human attributes and emotions. These gods represent a variety of created things or aspects of creation: life, death, order, chaos, war, fertility, harvest, famine, the sun, and the moon.

However, these versions of polytheistic religion use a God of the Gaps approach, where ancient people attempt to explain the operation of our world originating in creation by these deities.[133] Polytheism appears to be a more complex system of divine interaction between man and gods in sacrificial systems that allows mankind to satisfy and control supernatural powers. Could these proto-religions be distortions of the deeper truth that one God did create this cosmos? If so, this leaves open the question about the nature of God. And, if He created the universe, how does it function given various levels of His involvement? These are questions about what constitutes a religion and the rational process to examine and communicate religion. This book shows that Christianity offers the best answer to these questions.

---

[132] Taylor, C. (2009). A Secular Age. Harvard university press.
[133] Gleiser, M. (2014). The Island of Knowledge: The Limits of Science and the Search for Meaning. United States: Basic Books.

Atheism is a categorical denial that God exists and even the claim that the concept of God is incoherent.[134] But "The fool says in his heart, there is no God" (Psalm 14:1). Atheism is distinct from agnosticism which is the claim that one lacks knowledge enough to determine whether God exists.[135] Agnosticism is a more honest position expressing human limitations, but it is often used as a version of atheism-lite. This mild form of atheism is respectable and plausibly puts a person in a state of analysis while scanning the world for viable solutions to the biggest problems we face, questions about our origin, identity, purpose, morality, and destiny.[136,137] In many ways, all people are agnostic until they either believe or reject God. Hardened agnostics hold onto the threads of doubt. Some retain their confusion until the end of their lives, stubbornly refusing to accept the implications of the alternative.

Paul explains the mistaken religious instinct to cover our bases, "As I was going through your city, I saw the objects you worship. I found an altar that had these words written on it: to a god who is not known. You worship a god that you don't know, and this is the God I am telling you about! The God who made the whole world and everything in it is the Lord of the land and the sky. He does not live in temples built by human hands. This God is the One who gives life, breath, and everything else to people. He does not need any help from them; he has everything he needs. God began by making one person, and from him came

---

[134] Zenk, T. (2013). New atheism. The Oxford handbook of atheism, 245-262.
[135] Lightman, B. (2019). The Origins of Agnosticism: Victorian Unbelief and the Limits of Knowledge. United States: Johns Hopkins University Press.
[136] Colson, C. (2012). The Good Life. United States: Tyndale House Publishers, Incorporated.
[137] Wilkens, S., Sanford, M. L. (2009). Hidden Worldviews: Eight Cultural Stories That Shape Our Lives. United Kingdom: InterVarsity Press.

all the different people who live everywhere in the world. God decided exactly when and where they must live. God wanted them to look for him and perhaps search all around for him and find him, though he is not far from any of us" (Acts 17: 23-27). However, this religious mindset has diminished in Western Civilization. Over the last 200 years, throughout Europe and America, the secular view of life has risen in prominence to what many would call the default setting of our modern culture.

Charles Taylor (b. 1931), professor of philosophy at the University of Toronto, in his seminal book *A Secular Age*, explains, "A whole gamut of positions, from the most militant atheism to the most orthodox traditional theisms, passing through every possible position on the way, are represented and defended somewhere in our society." We have embraced religious pluralism, the idea that many religions can peacefully coexist. The more you emphasize the commonality between religions the more you blur the lines of distinction between them. However, no matter what attempts are made to blur the lines, real and profound differences between religions remain.

In a common religious understanding, humans attempt to reconcile life and death by seeking an afterlife and asking God to grant us admission into His everlasting paradise. This idea of life after death is consistent across religions. *Jannah* in Islam is the final resting place of righteous believers, translated as "paradise" or "garden."[138] Christianity is firmly rooted in a Judaic vision of heaven and resurrection which motivates and drives us. "He has made everything beautiful in its time. He has also set eternity in the human heart; yet no one can fathom what God has done

---

[138] Heaven, Hell, and the Afterlife: Eternity in Judaism, Christianity, and Islam [3 Volumes]: Eternity in Judaism, Christianity, and Islam. (2013). United States: ABC-CLIO.

from beginning to end" (Ecclesiastes 3:10-11). Jesus claimed to provide the fulfillment of the promise of resurrection, "This is the will of Him who sent Me, that of all that He has given Me I lose nothing but raise it up on the last day" (John 6:39). His validation by God through his resurrection was also a down payment on heaven for us, "But in fact Christ has been raised from the dead, the first fruits of those who have fallen asleep" (1 Corinthians 15:20). These are deeper truths about where human souls are going after death and attend all religious speculation about spiritual matters. Christianity's answers pull truth from religion to shape our understanding of the afterlife.

Many people struggle to reconcile the common human sense of their spiritual immortality with the consequences of a divine eternal judgment and its finality. Throughout time immemorial humans from Pharaohs to Vikings have tried to secure their place in a spiritual afterlife. Author Yuval Harari (b. 1976) assumed that religion and ideology are equally forms of manipulation and asked, "How do you cause people to believe in an imagined order such as Christianity, democracy, or capitalism?"[139] He believes that religious people who refuse to admit that their faith is a fantasy maintain a delusion. Richard Dawkins, in *The God Delusion*, offers this same nonsense when he writes, "Do you mean to tell me the only reason you try to be good is to gain God's approval and reward or to avoid his disapproval and punishment? That's not morality, that's just sucking up, apple-polishing, looking over your shoulder at the great surveillance camera in the sky, or the still small wiretap inside your head, monitoring your every move, even your every

---

[139] Harari, Y. N. (2014). Sapiens. A Brief History of Humankind. Yuval Noah Harari.

base thought."[140] Is your conscience lying to you about your need for a savior? "They show that the work of the law is written on their hearts, while their conscience also bears witness, and their conflicting thoughts accuse or even excuse them" (Romans 2:15).

If the United States were to do away with an imagined God and heaven, then there is no need for morality, judgment, or forgiveness. Despite their best efforts, no philosopher has devised a coherent ethical system on atheism. This resulting nihilism is rarely advocated by atheists. Efforts to deny the supernatural serve to separate humans from their spiritual moorings, leaving us adrift in the ocean of secularism. Yet, the religious instinct in 95 percent of the earth's population is toward belief.[141] We cannot avoid the reality that the object of religion is God.

True Impact

Religion has greatly impacted the progress of Western Civilization.[142] But sheer popularity does make religion valid. We may still ask if theism is true, then which religion is correct? Others have ably dealt with this question, sufficient to make the case that Christianity is true with a high degree of certainty.[143] Apologetic arguments build a foundation for theism, yet the weight of sociological impact of religion should not be used as an end-run around the logical case for faith. By stipulating that

---

[140] Cragun, R. T. (2015). Who are the "new atheists"?. In Atheist identities-spaces and social contexts (pp. 195-211). Springer, Cham.

[141] Bullivant, S., Farias, M., Lanman, J., & Lee, L. (2019). Understanding Unbelief: Atheists and agnostics around the world.

[142] Martin, M. (1991). The Case Against Christianity. United States: Temple University Press.

[143] Beckwith, Francis J., Craig, William Lane, Moreland, J. P. (2009) To Everyone an Answer: A Case for the Christian Worldview. United States: InterVarsity Press.

the case for Christianity is strong, we can examine the landscape of religion. Then we can compare these competing religions from an analytical and sociological standpoint. *The Constantine Doctrine* describes the impact of early Christian leadership on Western Civilization. What we find is that belief in God is the default setting and modifications in worldview take place on the margins. A significant proportion of the world affirms theism. This frames the likelihood that theism is correct and leads one to decide which religion is true.

The three great monotheistic religions affirm a single deity: Islam, Christianity, and Judaism. These influential systems of belief emerged in this order, Judaism (~1500 BC) then Christianity (~33 BC), and finally Islam (~610 BC). All three stem from the lineage of Abraham and the land of Canaan in the Middle East, now in present-day Israel or what certain Arabs claim as Palestine. Today, the largest branches of eastern religion are part of the Asian development of moral and meditative practices. Hinduism (polytheistic) and Buddhism (pantheistic or panentheistic) represent significant populations across the globe and adherents have been described as infidels or pagans by monotheistic believers. This is because the monotheistic religions clearly and overtly have rejected polytheism as false idolatry. The worldwide percentages of adherents are below.

Size of Major Religious Groups, 2015	
Religion	Percent
Christianity	31.2%
Islam	24.1%
Unaffiliated	16%
Hinduism	15.1%
Buddhism	6.9%
Folk Religions	5.7%
Other (includes Judaism, Bahá'í, Sikhism, and Jainism)	1.0%
Pew Research Center, 2015	

Christianity is overwhelmingly the largest religion in the world in terms of followers. In 2015, Pew Research estimated that there are nearly 2.4 billion Christians, about one-third of the world population, mainly divided among the Catholic, Protestant, and Eastern Orthodox groups. Today 65 percent of the US population calls themselves Christian.[144] Many Americans say that they believe in the Bible but in a recent survey "a majority (54%) unwilling to define human life as sacred and half claiming that the Bible is ambiguous in its teaching about abortion."[145] Not every person who affiliates with a religion adheres to its teachings. There is a difference between nominal belief, which amounts to joining a social club without real commitment, and imperfect people who are truly redeemed and "work out your salvation with fear and trembling" (Philippians 2:12). Declaring

---

[144] https://www.pewforum.org/2019/10/17/in-u-s-decline-of-christianity-continues-at-rapid-pace
[145] https://www.arizonachristian.edu/culturalresearchcenter/research/ AWVI 2020: Churches and Worldview (Report #11: 10-06-2020)

that the Bible gives strict restrictions on sin will get you labeled as an extremist. Some academics attribute your closed-minded behavior to tribalism. In one sense, standing up for the truth will create an us-versus-them mentality, however, this is only a result of one party's intransigent, stubborn refusal to accept the truth.

Religion is not true because most people are religious. That is an argument *ad populum*. However, the overwhelming percentage of spiritual beliefs is a statistical reality. Apologetics help to weigh arguments and evidence for the existence of God. Since theism is accepted as true by most of the world's population it follows that our sense of the eternal and moral world reflects reality. We perceive our soul the way we sense gravity. But some claim that instinct of justice and authority may only be an aspect of human psychology. Many may question the truth of theism, which is outside of the purview of this book, but most people self-report that they believe in God. Therefore, a movement to abandon faith and reject God required an argument that overcomes the general acceptance of a created order, supreme being, and eternal heaven.

Evidence for the existence of God is independent of these social statistics. And the trend toward secularization leads many to conclude that belief in God will be reduced in the future. Many scholars claim that a lack of education is correlated with religion and that human beings will educate themselves away from belief. However, the reason why people do or do not believe in God is confounded by a multitude of variables including morality, language, and culture. And religion is positively correlated with education.[146,147] Therefore, our concept of

---

[146] Murray, C. (2012). Coming Apart: The State of White America, 1960-2010. United States: Crown Publishing Group.
[147] Schwadel, P. (2011). The effects of education on Americans' religious practices, beliefs, and affiliations. Review of Religious Research, 53(2), 161-182.

God is deeply rooted in our notion of creation and judgment tied to our sense of law and justice. Humans seek to live a good life because our conscience convicts us of a pending judgment. This guilt and shame complex is shared throughout all cultures in the world. Again, the Bible addresses this intrinsic need of human beings. "And no creature is hidden from his sight, but all are naked and exposed to the eyes of him to whom we must give account" (Hebrews 4:13).

Homo sapiens have a religious instinct built into our self or psyche or spirit that is hardwired into our DNA or brain or mind. We believe that we are more than our flesh. This is mind-body dualism.[148] Christianity endorses a spiritual view of life where the human soul is durable and eternal. Religion has always offered an explanation for the afterlife. This is reflected in a moral expectation for justice and reward after death. Joseph Campbell (1904-1987), an author on spirituality and religion, in his book *The Hero with a Thousand Faces,* made the argument that the similarity between religions is the result of some severely buried psycho-historical needs. This archetypal Jungian approach to religion, developed by Carl Jung (1875- 1961) a Swiss psychoanalyst, is promoted by the likes of modern academic psychologists like Jordan Peterson (b. 1962), a Canadian clinical psychologist and self-help guru. However, could the commonalities of certain aspects of religions speak to a common root story based in fact while also highlighting profound differences? They all address fundamental topics such as origin, morality, and destiny but do so very differently. These differences could make the case for one single source of truth by triangulating the various perspectives.

---

[148] Bendelow, G., & Williams, S. (1995). Pain and the mind-body dualism: a sociological approach. Body & Society, 1(2), 83-103.

If all religions refer to the idea of God's moral law, it makes sense that at least one God exists.[149] If all religions reference creation mythology, it is logical that we should be able to confirm through science the beginning of the universe.[150] Mythology is the study of historical and moral truths contained in stories. This is very different from a modern myth which itself is not propositional or prescriptive truth. A story does not tell us exactly what happened or what we should do about it, instead, it invites us to put ourselves in that story that all our forebearers also faced. If all religions seek to impose a moral order, it follows that we are moral creatures endowed with a conscience. If every religion attempts to reconcile our eternal soul with an afterlife, then maybe we have something to worry about besides dying. These patterns require a more comprehensive explanation than the benefits of storytelling to communal groups. That is circular reasoning.

In comparison, the Hindu religion existed for centuries before Siddharta Gautama "Buddha"(c. 563-483 BC) created a branch of religion that his followers called Buddhism (483 BC) in southern Nepal. The language, grammar, and morphology of Sanskrit reflect the religious transition of this era. Buddhism claims that "the root of suffering is neither the feeling of pain nor of sadness nor even of meaninglessness. Rather, the real root of suffering is this never-ending and pointless pursuit of ephemeral feelings, which causes us to be in a constant state of tension, restlessness, and dissatisfaction."[151] These ascetic impulses were

---

[149] Craig, W. L., Wielenberg, E. J. (2020). A Debate on God and Morality: What is the Best Account of Objective Moral Values and Duties?. United States: Taylor & Francis.

[150] Craig, W. L. (2000). The Kalam cosmological argument. Wipf and Stock Publishers.

[151] Ibid. Harrari

shared by Jesus Christ who said, "Foxes have dens and birds have nests, but the Son of Man has no place to lay his head" (Luke 9:58). The Christian tradition of rejecting the need for creature comforts is found in John the Baptist, Paul, Origen, Jerome, and Augustine and can be traced back to Judaism but are distinct from Greek traditions.[152] However, most Christians lived life within the tension of the here and now and the eternal, which is tension between the material and spiritual.

Therefore, an operational definition of religion is the practice of worship that links the transcendent, supernatural, and metaphysical. It is our sense of the divine that motivates our ethical practice. The great German Lutheran philosopher Immanuel Kant (1724-1804) revered *achtung*, practical reason as if it overpowered base instinct, emotion, and desire. Deontology bases morality on universal rules, which is an expression of natural law and absolute truth. Yet, if we were to worship human reason as a law-giving ability, our society would become rife with antinomianism, which is the belief that man is a law unto himself. This is because human beings are not perfectly rational. Each person's reason, however imperfect and corrupted by sin, gives rise to their twisted morality.

---

[152] Richard Finn (2009). Asceticism in the Graeco-Roman World. Cambridge University Press. pp. 94–97.

6

Rising Atheism

RETURNING TO BLAISE Pascal he recommended that when considering God's existence, we should, "wager, then, without hesitation that He is... There is here an infinity of an infinitely happy life to gain, a chance of gain against a finite number of chances of loss, and what you stake is finite." This is not an argument for the existence of God, but a strategy when dealing with uncertainty. In contrast, Michael Shermer (b. 1954), a religious skeptic and science author, like Bertrand Russel (1872-1970), a prominent British atheist, mathematician, and philosopher, explains his unbelief in a hypothetical conversation with a God he denies, "Lord, I did the best I could with the tools you granted me ... I tried to do unto others as I would have them do unto me, and although I fell far short of this ideal far too many times, I tried to apply your foundational principle whenever I could. Whatever the nature of your immortal and infinite spiritual essence is, as a mortal finite corporeal being I cannot possibly fathom it despite my best efforts, and so do with me what you will." He throws himself at the mercy of an unknown God with a soft appeal to his goodness. This atheist/agnostic wager assumes that God doesn't care who accepts him as Lord and instead considers your deeds to determine who goes to heaven or hell. It is the same version of theism that most pagans had, and many works-based Christians still have.

Sam Harris (b. 1967), a prominent neuroscientist, and atheist, believes that one should live according to some overarching standards of love, tolerance, and compassion "to make the world a better place." These people have no grounds for these moral principles and confuse moral epistemology with moral practice. This is related to the "is" versus "ought" or facts-values debate where prescriptive rules are not derived from descriptive facts about the world, but our moral duties and values refer to a higher law. Most philosophers affirm objective morality. In doing so we affirm God's role as the ultimate lawgiver.

Too many people are confused about the standards that guide our society and thus accede to norms defined by their preferences. If Satan promotes amorality (the absence or negation of morality) rather than immorality, the purpose is to increase the freedom humans have from their conscience and thus increase their sin. Antinomianism is a reoccurring heresy that advocates the removal of laws so that libertinism will prevail. It is important to recognize that Satan plans to promote the spiritual, then moral, then psychological, then intellectual, rejection of God. He revels in our wickedness knowing that the further we fall into self-harming despair the less likely our return will be. For every person who hits rock bottom only to be saved and who can share their testimony of God's grace many persist in their sin and die in their trespasses.

Further atheists confound the idea of salvation with works. This is a common problem for all religious people. This was the primary theological issue that led to the Protestant Reformation and persists to this day within the church. Humans too often attempt to reach God with our efforts. The temptation is to believe that the positive impact we have on family and friends will be judged to overpower every sin contemplated, word uttered, and act committed. But evil is the privation of good. Inherent in the rejection of evil is a standard of goodness. This is highlighted by the Euthyphro Dilemma which asks whether something is good because God calls it good or is independent of God's decree. However, as we will see, atheists who take this tact are appealing to the benevolence of a God that they disbelieve. If they assume that there is a God and He is benevolent, then he has adequately revealed himself in creation and history. It is therefore God's moral character that is the paradigm of goodness.

Paganism is a version of polytheism that worships humanistic or animalistic deities, categorized as a deviation from true religion by reformation and enlightenment thinkers alike.[153] This instinct to imbue creation with the powers of a creator, however misplaced, is a significant aspect of the human religious nature tampered with by sin. "They exchanged the truth about God for a lie and worshiped and served created things rather than the Creator..." (Romans 1:25). Baltic pagans worshiped idols in sacred groves and fields, practiced human sacrifice, buried animals alive at funerals and their grim shrines were served by priests.[154] These death cult practitioners were often derogatorily referred to as heathens. Desires to placate divine wrath, appeal to divine capriciousness, or manipulate God are the basis of idolatry.

These are prototypical versions of a nonscientific grasp of a natural phenomenon. Rather than thinking of creation as operating outside of God's direct intervention, Christians believe that God's sovereignty is over every decision made by humans. Christianity espouses a creator-creation distinction that affirms God's omnipotence, omniscience, and omnipresence while He allows much of earthly events to occur without his

---

[153] Horák, P. (2016). The Image of Paganism in the Age of Reason: From idolatry towards a secular concept of polytheism. Pomegranate: The International Journal of Pagan Studies, volume 18, issue: 2.

[154] Seward, D. (1974). The monks of war. Paladin.

involvement.[155] A fatalistic view of creation becomes deterministic religious practice when man's desire to understand, even control, or appeal to these distant transcendent powers becomes the purpose of communion with God. But this only makes sense if you see yourself as a spiritual being who can reach a higher or deeper reality. You either see ghosts or gods as other minds or God gave us a sense of the spiritual realm. Hume argued that "these ideas are, perhaps, too far stretched; but still it must be acknowledged that, by representing the Deity as so intelligible and comprehensible, and so similar to a human mind, we are guilty of the grossest and most narrow partiality and make ourselves the model of the whole universe."[156] This same accusation can apply to religion in general, man may make himself the object of religion rather than God.

The term *apophenia* was invented by German neurologist Klaus Conrad (1905-1961) to describe the way that humans often perceive connections between unrelated events or objects. He speculated that this condition was a precursor to schizophrenia. Like our view of other minds, our understanding of causality either drives us toward God or away from Him. At its basic form cause and effect is a fundamental principle of the universe. How we view God's role in causing or allowing events will impact our understanding of His character. Do we think that God is a divine puppet master pulling our strings for his amusement? Can we experience God on a personal level through prayer or other spiritual practices? Do we share this image of the divine mind imprinted in ourselves, which reflects our rationality? If so, we begin to see God as the intentional source of the universe

---

[155] Fergusson, D. (2014). Creation. Wm. B. Eerdmans Publishing.
[156] Hume, D. (1779). Dialogues concerning natural religion. William Blackwood.

in every decision we make, for when we exercise free will we are most like our creator. If God freely chose to create this cosmos, then we can freely choose to believe in Him and live accordingly or discard Him.

Atheistic psychologists have attempted to explain away the human belief in a deity as a projection of our mind onto another. Do we simply think that there must be an ultimate mind because we believe our consciousness is evidence of a mind that is independent of our physical body? Is spirit or psyche just another name for our mind? Ludwig Feuerbach an avowed atheist, wrote, "The divine being is nothing else than the human being, or rather, the human nature purified, freed from the limits of the individual man, made objective—i.e., contemplated and revered as another, a distinct being. All the attributes of the divine nature are, therefore, attributes of the human nature."[157] But, this has the causal arrow reversed. Because we are like God we aspire to be like God. We have a spirit and desire the purification of our soul to live in a harmonious relationship with the God we have been disconnected from.

The Jewish Austrian neurologist Sigmund Freud determined that "at bottom God is nothing other than an exalted father."[158] However, his rivalry with his genial father may mean that atheism is "an illusion caused by the Oedipal desire to kill the father (God) and replace him with oneself."[159] To the father of psychoanalysis and many of his progeny, God is not real. He only is the name we give to the source of our guilt and shame when our

---

[157] Feuerbach, L. (1957). The Essence of Christianity. 1841. Trans. George Eliot. New York: Harper.

[158] Freud, S., & Breuer, J. (2001). The standard edition of the complete psychological works of Sigmund Freud (Vol. 2). Random House.

[159] Vitz, P. C. (2013). Faith of the fatherless: The psychology of atheism. Ignatius Press.

conscience is pricked by the pains of our sin. Freud defrauded his projection theory from the grand skeptic David Hume, "All the sentiments of the human mind, gratitude, resentment, love, friendship, approbation, blame, pity, emulation, envy, have a plain reference to the state and situation of man, and are calculated for preserving the existence and promoting the activity of such a being in such circumstances. It seems, therefore, unreasonable to transfer such sentiments to a supreme existence or to suppose him actuated by them…" Hume provided many deists a judgment against the reasonableness of God, we irrationally transfer our desire for ideals on God. Hume was uncomfortable with a God who seems to share our emotions as well as our rationality. Of course, all these critiques of religion refer to theism but were made in a distinctly Christian culture. Plantinga points out that "These a-theological arguments are as unsuccessful as the arguments from natural theology… to the question, 'Are religious beliefs rationally justified?'"[160] He points out that the warrant of evidence leads to the proper conclusion: God exists.

The Science of Theism

Subsequently, psychologist Jonathan Haidt suspects that divinity is an aspect of human nature that is real regardless of whether or not God exists. We aspire to moral goodness and Haidt calls that feeling of warmth and desire to become better "elevation." This type of thinking is typical of secularism. An atheist like Haidt attempts to create a new psychological construct, develop a theory, and test it in experiments rather than acknowledging the most logical source of these feelings, a

---

[160] Plantinga, A. (1990). God and other minds: A study of the rational justification of belief in God. Cornell University Press.

real God who does exist and motivates this feeling in our souls (which Haidt denies). Therefore, this essential belief in God is properly basic, i.e., a brute fact, such as the belief that other people, the outside world, and history exist.[161] God imposes Himself on the human mind the same way our past and family impact our lives. He is inescapable.

Someone who denies any of these facts would be certifiably insane. For example, no one walks around with the belief that other people are a figment of their imagination. This form of philosophy is called solipsism and it is universally condemned. But many opponents of religion sow seeds of doubt about the nature of reality at the academic and popular levels. The effort to understand how our minds exist and think is called the philosophy of mind.[162] The project of this discipline is very different from that of psychology. Descartes with his famous claim *Cogito Ego Sum* "I think therefore I am" provided one irrefutable philosophical truth that has given rise to this area of study over the last 200 years. Therefore, all humans know that they exist, and thus other people exist. Plantinga states, "…if my belief in other minds is rational, so is my belief in God. But obviously the former is rational; so, therefore, is the latter."[163] Simply put, God is the ultimate spirit, an unembodied mind, and thus our acceptance that a world of minds exists is drawn from our acceptance of God's being.

How should we consider personal experience as part of religion? William Lane Craig described the inner witness of the Holy Spirit as a rational argument for the existence of God, in

---

[161] Plantinga, A. (1981). Is belief in God properly basic?. Noûs, 41-51.

[162] Chappell, V. C. (1962). The philosophy of mind.

[163] Plantinga, A. (1990). God and other minds: A study of the rational justification of belief in God. Cornell University Press.

a complementary collection of arguments for theism.[164] Rather than building upon one another like a house of cards, like chain-mail armor these arguments and evidences provide additional strength that binds to one another. Alvin Plantinga (b. 1932), the consummate modern Christian professor of philosophy at Notre Dame University, references some forty-two arguments for the existence of God. The counterargument to personal experience is to appeal to the general human experience of the mundane. Hume's argument which addressed doubts and fostered skepticism starts with this premise, "Our ideas reach no farther than our experience: We have no experience of divine attributes and operations." However, our life starts with the miracle of our birth and continues in twists and turns that individuals throughout history attribute to divine intervention starting with the light of conscience convicting us of our sin.

Social science can tell us a lot about the attitudes, beliefs, and opinions of a group of people. While self-reported data is notoriously biased, these variations are consistent and able to be controlled for. Statistical tools, analysis, and inference are valid forms of mathematical reasoning. We can understand the bulk of the data and draw valid conclusions based on probability statistics. However, this does not represent a fulsome view of reality. In many ways, these instruments and findings can be skewed and doctored to color the outcomes and shape opinions rather than reflect reality. The way that we read reported data is very important. A trained social scientist knows the limitations and boundary conditions of research, they can ask the right questions about the methodology behind a study.

---

[164] Craig, W. L. (2008). Reasonable faith: Christian truth and apologetics. Crossway.

Many researchers intentionally do not attempt to falsify the findings that they agree with or want to promote. Most people do not have training in statistical analysis and therefore defer to experts to tell them what the findings of any study are. In doing so, the researcher can shape opinions because people tend to place themselves around the mean. For example, LaCour and Green published a study based on fabricated data indicating that political canvassers had great success in changing people's minds about gay marriage.[165] This never happened. Methodological atheism in social science perverts the tools used to collect data to irreligious ends.[166] Therefore, modern tools of social science need to be balanced with logic when it comes to extrapolating our understanding of religion in context.

Anthropology is built upon sociology, our understanding of the history of man comes from our study of groups. We see farms, pots, weapons, tools, and cities and speculate about who these people were. And we infer from artifacts the religious activity of people and groups. Pascal wrote, "When I consider the brief span of my life absorbed into the eternity which precedes and will succeed it... I take fright and am amazed to see myself here rather than there: there is no reason for me to be here rather than there, now rather than then. Who put me here? By whose command and act were this place and time allotted to me?"[167] Our lives are not accidents. The Prophet Daniel wrote of God, "He changes times and seasons; he removes kings and sets up kings; he gives wisdom to the wise and knowledge to those who

---

[165] https://www.chronicle.com/article/what-social-science-can-learn-from-the-lacour-scandal/?cid=gen_sign_in
[166] Beed, C., & Beed, C. (2015). Social Sin, Theology and Social Science. Journal of Catholic Social Thought, 12(2), 279-300.
[167] Ibid. Pascal, Blaise. Pensées...

have understanding" (Daniel 2:21). Our lives are in the hands of God, and He has ordained the location and purpose of each person and people group. The Constantine Doctrine holds that God sovereignly set up the conditions and situations where leaders like Constantine the Great would rise and, if needed, God may even intervene in human history.

As these early hunter/gatherer societies show us, people tend to benefit from working together and thus create cities. In cities, greater order is needed, and all activities are shaped by organizing features of group action. One such activity is the worship of God, which when organized tends to orient people in the same direction. The state will always be linked to religion. We create governments to instill order. We need to worship a power greater than ourselves; ideally, we worship the God who created us. But people tend to fill that void, that God-shaped hole, with all kinds of things. Some people seek power themselves; others worship the idols of sex, money, and fame. We instead may praise our athletes, thespians, or politicians. Anything that is a counterfeit god will lead us away from the one true God.[168] But true religion points us to God.

---

[168] Keller, T. (2011). Counterfeit gods: The empty promises of money, sex, and power, and the only hope that matters. Penguin.

7

A Christian Worldview

RELIGIONS AND MODERN ideologies compete for the same ground, our minds. And the more we can understand the role that worldview plays in our public discourse the better we can communicate the great truths of scripture. The amalgamation of individuals' opinions in a society lays the foundation for government. Therefore, it is necessary to see the connections between theology and public policy. Our worldview, derived from the term *Weltanschauung* coined by Kant, is "an intellectual conception of the universe from the perspective of a human knower."[169] Worldview is the term that many Christians have embraced to describe the general and accepted practical philosophy of every person in action. It is the lens through which we see the world.[170]

Philosophy sparks great questions and theology offers powerful answers. Isaiah Berlin (1909-1997), a Russian-British political scientist, once described the costs and benefits of philosophy, "You avert your gaze and try to get the responsibility up from your own to some broader back, state, or church, or class, or some other association to which you belong, perhaps to the general moral code of ordinary decent people. But shouldn't

---

[169] Naugle, D. Worldview: The History of a Concept; Eerdmans: Cambridge, UK, 2002.
[170] Kant, I.; Gregor, M.J. Critique of Judgment; Hackett: Indianapolis, IN, 1790 (pp. 111–112).

you think the problem through yourself?"[171] Everyone has a worldview, that unique combination of their philosophy and theology. This sense-making apparatus is influenced by the media we consume and the ideas we contemplate.[172] We need a group of particularly curious individuals as philosophers to ask uncomfortable questions and provoke us to think, if only for a moment, about the deeper reasons why we do what we do. And we need pastors, teachers, preachers, and prophets to give us true answers to these difficult questions. Then we can go on living and acting accordingly to better examine our beliefs and values. Philosophy can and should be the *ancilla theologiae,* the handmaiden to theology, leading us toward truth.

A worldview has been described as a combination of each person's axiology (the study of values alone, under the philosophical branch of ethics studying moral principles in duties and values), ontology (the study of existence), epistemology (the study of knowledge), praxeology (the study of action), and cosmology (the study of the universe, origin,).[173] This may be an overly complicated way to say, our worldview is the sum of the way that we see and experience the world. Throughout history, this view has been shaped and directed by religion. Natural theology provides arguments for the existence of God through reason and evidence.[174] The Christian worldview is the most comprehensive one provided by any religion or ideology.

---

[171] Magee, B. (2001). Talking philosophy: dialogues with fifteen leading philosophers. United Kingdom: Oxford University Press.

[172] Weick, K. E. (1995). Sensemaking in organizations (Vol. 3). Sage.

[173] Koltko-Rivera, M. E. (2004). The psychology of worldviews. Review of general psychology, 8(1), 3-58.

[174] Chignell, Andrew; Pereboom, Derk (2020), "Natural Theology and Natural Religion", in Zalta, Edward N. (ed.), The Stanford Encyclopedia of Philosophy (Fall 2020 ed.), Metaphysics Research Lab, Stanford University.

However, throughout Western Civilization people have challenged the claims of Christianity. This balance between allowing questions and doubt, even encouraging free-thinking people to reject faith, and protecting the faithful from false teaching has proven extremely difficult to achieve. David Hume (1711-1776), the oft-reprimanded Scottish skeptic, posited through his characters that, "It is only as a science, replied Demea, subjected to human reasoning and disputation, that I postpone the study of natural theology."[175] To some extent, we can forgive Hume's impetuous nature and raucous empiricism. He was ignorant of many of the scientific developments that verify the facts of creation and history we have in the Twenty-first Century which validate many claims in scripture. Christianity still makes supernatural claims, posits miracles, which even when true are impossible to verify just like natural events in history, and offers scripture which reflects prophecy outside our everyday experience. But his desire to put God in a test-tube as it were, and study religion as a science, mistakes the nature and purpose of religion.

Some claim the merger of the Roman Empire with the Christian church was the inevitable march of religion through history. But this view mistakes the significance and direction of this event. It began a process of rationalizing the supernatural, building science upon theology, and organizing the legal statutes of civilization. Many people recoil at the way that Christian victims were replaced with oppressors over the next century and a half. But this view mistakes the acquisition of power with its misuse. Many Christians were attacked because they attempted to

---

[175] Hume, D. (1779). Dialogues Concerning Natural Religion. United Kingdom: William Blackwood.

reform mores and behavior. The church was altered irrevocably in the years following Constantinian rule. Power was consolidated in Rome and later distributed to Constantinople. Wealth was generated through trade, accrued to some landed men, and prisoners were used by slave masters, and these practices grew across Europe.[176] Faithfulness was found in pockets. Faithlessness prevailed in others. Worldliness competed with godliness and many succumbed to the allure of material and control.

Bishops became more powerful. Pagan priests and rulers had rights, freedoms, and privileges. Certain people received tax exemptions. Constantine implemented piecemeal changes where the *decurions*, Roman mayors and governors, slowly were removed or converted themselves. Judges became Christianized through the church. The former *diositin* regional governance model was adopted by the church. Hierarchy added influence through concentric circles through the papacy. The split between the Eastern and Western divisions was rife with problems, and the mixture of spiritual and political authority presented new problems. This is reflected in the use of some pagan architecture, such as the basilica, in Christian cathedrals. But the goal was the integration of culture to transform souls.

Christianity became more open to movement between the world and the church. The City of God and Man began interacting. The boundaries between the sacred and profane became more permeable as greater interaction between them took place. Julian the Apostate ruled for two years and was roundly rejected by the Roman people. The Council of Nicaea (325) enacted by Constantine opposed Arian heresy and Gnostic Docetism (a

---

[176] Harper, K. (2011). Slavery in the Late Roman World, AD 275–425. (n.p.): Cambridge University Press.

claim that Christ only seemed human).[177] Previous councils such as the Jerusalem Council addressed church doctrine and resolved certain conflicts. However, with Constantine initiating the first ecumenical council, the founding of the church was attached to the implied power of the Roman Empire. This meant that the ruling carried with it the political magisterium of the emperor. And, while the excommunication of Arians was not carried out or enforced by the throne, the threat or pressure to conform was pronounced. This continued into the Middle Ages.

Today, many medieval Christians in books and films are characterized as religious zealots, base hypocrites, or weak priests. Some men of the cloth are portrayed hiding behind robes or dying as martyrs instead of being celebrated as either brave or compassionate men. Too often in these movies, we see doubting, vile, and sad men claiming Christ who fight viciously for blood and treasure instead of for their faith and family. Granted, some men who claimed the name of Christ violated important Biblical moral codes. Battle requires harsh survival tactics and everyone sins. But if that is hypocrisy, then even regenerate Christians' sins are never forgiven. Rarely do we see an accurate portrayal of a faithful man, who may have his doubts, yet persists in his faith and acts courageously and with great strength to protect his family and land to the glory of God. This is not some phantasma, a fake construct of revision history written by victors. Real men fought, bled, and died for a cause greater than themselves, the gospel, and the cross of Christ. There is a beautiful and true story of religion to be found in our history.

---

[177] Ridgeon, Lloyd V. J. (2001). Ridgeon, Lloyd V. J. (ed.). Islamic Interpretations of Christianity. Palgrave Macmillan. ISBN 978-0-312-23854-4. Retrieved 25 April 2012.

American Evangelicalism

Thomas Jefferson (1743-1826) is a good example of an intelligent man who struggled to reconcile the supernatural and divine claims of Jesus Christ. Jefferson was essentially a Unitarian Deist, who eschewed labeling his belief system.[178] He had affections for the Christian faith and moral teaching of Jesus but didn't adhere to the religion as stringently as many other founding fathers.[179] However, by today's standards, he would be considered religious. The so-called "Jefferson Bible" was never meant to replace the Bible but supplement it. Jefferson wrote a letter to Benjamin Rush (1746-1813) which serves as a preface.[180] In it, he outlines his objections to philosophers, Jews, and Jesus. He stated, "Hence the doctrines which he delivered were defective as a whole, and fragments only of what he did deliver have come to us mutilated, misstated, and often unintelligible."[181] This is common among intellectuals; they have a hard time dealing with their own limitations. But Jefferson is wrong about the gospels and Jesus. While speaking in parables may be misunderstood, the things that he said clearly are simply hard to accept. "This is why I speak to them in parables: 'Though seeing, they do not see; though hearing, they do not hear or understand.' In them the prophecy of Isaiah is fulfilled: 'You will be

---

[178] Coulter, M. L., Throckmorton, W. (2012). Getting Jefferson Right: Fact Checking Claims about Our Third President. United States: Salem Grove Press.

[179] Barton, D. (2012). The Jefferson Lies: Exposing the Myths You've Always Believed About Thomas Jefferson. United States: Thomas Nelson.

[180] https://founders.archives.gov/documents/Jefferson/01-40-02-0178-0002 retrived on Nov. 1, 2020.

[181] Holowchak, M. A. (2018). Thomas Jefferson's Bible. In Thomas Jefferson's Bible. De Gruyter.

ever hearing but never understanding; you will be ever seeing but never perceiving'" (Matthew 13:14).

Too often geniuses attempt to cover over their misunderstandings with fancy words. No matter their mental capacity, deficits in human thinking often emerge because our reason is flawed. Humans are not perfectly rational. But a God who cares and loves for human beings is more perfect than the deist's mechanical watchmaker.[182] He can illuminate our souls and enrapture our minds with the truth of His word. Jefferson's letter to the Danbury Baptist church congregation was a pledge that the wall between church and state would prevent the government from taking over the church, not the other way around. He never wanted to substitute his doubts for their faith. Thomas Paine (1737-1809) shared Jefferson's struggles and wrote, "I have now gone through the Bible, as a man would go through a wood with an ax on his shoulder and fell trees. Here they lie; and the priests, if they can, may replant them. They may, perhaps, stick them in the ground, but they will never make them grow."[183] He was another revolutionary thinker who was disturbed by God's revolution. But even Paine joined The Society of Theophilanthropists dedicated to "promote morality, religious toleration, and a belief in one God."[184] Good men cannot avoid the goodness of God.

However, the debate over the intent of the founder's words vis-a-vis the church masks why they believed it was important. Members of what should be called the universal Christian church, rather than any specific denomination, played a significant part

[182] Leftow, B. (2011). Why perfect being theology?. International Journal for Philosophy of Religion, 69(2), 103-118.
[183] Paine, T. (1795). The Age of Reason, Part First (1794). Part II.
[184] Paine, T. (1875). The Age of Reason: Being an Investigation of True and Fabulous Theology. United States: Josiah P. Mendum.

in our nation's founding. This idea of an ecumenical universal catholic church is important to promoting a common understanding of both orthodoxy and heterodoxy. The word catholic technically comes from the Greek phrase *catholicus* which means "on the whole" or "in general." The term adopted by the Catholic church was meant to denote completeness and unity. We know, "...the dead, small and great, stand before God; and the books were opened: and another book was opened, which is of life: and the dead were judged out of those things which were written in the books, according to their works" (Revelation 20:12). All Christians still believe in the universal church; we only differ on where it is found. Anyone, of any stripe or creed, can be born again, thus the Church is the collection of believers known by God who abide in Christ throughout history and this world.

There are many Christians that have bought into the idea that religion is a private faith. By rightly accepting the individualized and personal nature of our belief we can make a mistake. Just because there is no collective salvation and you are not saved because you are a member of a tribe, group, or race, that does not mean that we are not called to influence the public sphere. You can share your faith with people that you meet and in doing so transform a nation. This process of evangelism in word and deed aids the preparation of a cultural *milieu* that is more amenable to Christian leaders. Europe is proof positive as a counter-example. By ridiculing and condemning faithful Christians many countries in the continent have made it more difficult for younger generations to accept the legitimacy of religious answers to existential questions. Church leaders say that we should evangelize, but many Christians admit that they do not. If our faith matters, we must become more outgoing and courageous in the way that we talk about God in public. We must not deny Jesus for the sake of getting along with others or use calls for civility to silence the Church.

Influencing culture is important. This can be done through politics, education, and entertainment. Compare the role of the pastor and statesman to a media executive. Secular ideas are promoted from our idea-centers in Los Angeles, New York City, and Washington, D.C. to people in the United States and around the world. The influence of secularism is growing, and we are not doing enough to counter these lies with the truths of scripture. Twisting grains of truth is a common tactic within intellectual and spiritual warfare. "Now the serpent was more crafty than any other beast of the field that the Lord God had made. He said to the woman, 'Did God say, "You shall not eat of any tree in the garden?"'" (Genesis 3:1). This shows us that we are responsible for the lies we believe and share. We must be people of truth. Accidentally or explicitly making false statements is wrong. And a partial truth can be a whole lie. A murder crafting an alibi may make truthful statements to conceal their crime. If they killed someone at 5:00 PM, they could honestly say, "I was home all night." But all these efforts at deception only serve to further cloud the thinking of ourselves and others. This same problem occurs in our dialog about religion and society.

Sohrab Ahmari (b. 1985) questioned the principles of David French (b. 1969), an attorney, evangelical Christian, and conservative columnist, when French stated, "The fact that a person can get a room in a library and hold a Drag Queen Story Hour and get people to come? That's one of the blessings of liberty."[185] Vincent Phillip Muñoz (b. 1976?), University of Notre Dame

---

[185] https://www.newyorker.com/news/the-political-scene/david-french-sohrab-ahmari-and-the-battle-for-the-future-of-conservatism

Associate Professor of Religion & Public Life objected and wrote, "French's federalism-enhanced procedural liberalism does not recognize the threat to America for what it is." He also explained that "Like Rawls, French eschews the natural law foundations of American republicanism, and thus he is unable to recognize the limits of freedom. His legal relativism led him into moral relativism."[186] This is the challenge to religious pluralism. The human need for God requires an ordered theology for us to worship properly. We can debate the finer points of religion, but an orthodox faith requires some authority of interpretation about what constitutes proper behavior.

This is what the Roman Catholic church attempts to provide, and about which protestant denominations differ greatly. Many people have reflected creedal statements in the most salient points of Christianity for the universal church. C.S. Lewis's (1898- 1963) *Mere Christianity* was a highly successful effort to outline the essential doctrines of the Christian faith and draw logical distinctions between natural theology, apologetics, and personal preferences. In it, he wrote, "That a great many things have gone wrong with the world that God made and that God insists, and insists very loudly, on our putting them right again."[187] Lewis addresses the deity of Jesus, "I'm ready to accept Jesus as a great moral teacher, but I don't accept his claim to be God. That is the one thing we must not say." He expanded on this point with the well-known Lord, Liar, or Lunatic Trilemma, to which we may add Legend (which is a collective lie). Likewise, Bob George (b. 1933) wrote the book *Classic Christianity* to describe the common features of orthodox expressions of the Christian faith. He writes,

---

[186] https://www.firstthings.com/article/2020/12/more-is-needed
[187] Lewis, C. S. (1952). Mere Christianity. United States: HarperCollins.

"Man was so engineered by God that the presence of the Creator within the creature is indispensable to his humanity" and "Truth sets you free. Error binds you."[188] The goal of these works is to clarify and unify the essential tenets of Christian doctrine.

In contrast, Michael Martin (1932-2015), an atheist professor of philosophy at Boston University, uses the term Basic Christianity to describe the core of the faith. Basic Christianity includes the belief that "a theistic God exists (*redundant*)... Jesus lived at the time of Pilate... Jesus is the incarnation of God... one is saved through faith in Jesus, and... Jesus is the model of ethical behavior."[189] In his book *The Case Against Christianity* (1991) he states the orthodox Christian believes in Basic Christianity plus believes in doctrines of "the Trinity, the Virgin Birth, the Crucifixion by Pilate, the Resurrection, and The Second Coming." Martin goes on to spectacularly fail in making a case against the historical reliability of the archeological facts of Christianity, let alone his mistreatment of the philosophical consistency within these doctrines.

In many ways, the Christian church in America has been fighting a rear-guard action. For too long we have been on a cultural retreat. If it is true that this nation is no longer very Christian, it is also true that it once was Christian. We will explore this in greater detail in the forthcoming books *The Columbus Initiative, The Lincoln Legacy,* and *The Reagan Compromise*. America has fallen away from the faith. America is less Christian in 2022 than it once was in 1780.[190] This leaves open the fact

---

[188] George, B. (2010). Classic Christianity. United States: Harvest House Publishers.

[189] Martin, M. (1993). The Case Against Christianity. United States: Temple University Press.

[190] Brown, C. G. (2009). The death of Christian Britain: understanding secularisation, 1800–2000. Routledge.

that even in a culture suffuse with moral values, individuals of varied faiths persist in sin, hating, murdering, lying, cheating, and stealing. And we need to admit our failures and forgiveness as a nation. We know, "if my people who are called by my name humble themselves and pray and seek my face and turn from their wicked ways, then I will hear from heaven and will forgive their sin and heal their land" (2 Chronicles 7:14). A massive revival when our hearts turn toward God is the ultimate answer to the cultural problems we face as a country.

Practicing Christians still struggle with unrepentant sin, and some may fall into habitual sin or moral failures that pain our souls. We may feel the need to cry out and look to Christ's return, "My soul is in anguish. How long, O Lord, how long?" (Psalm 6:3). Likewise, nominal Christians and those who are opposed to the church also come up short of God's righteous standards and miss the mark. We are defending our retreat and flank by attempting to preserve some semblance of reasonable religious exercise. Ronald Reagan famously said, "When our Founding Fathers passed the First Amendment, they sought to protect churches from government interference."[191] This was the original intent of the establishment clause. But our Bill of Rights was not meant to hide the Church from the world. It was meant to protect our ability to grow and thrive as the Church so that the gates of hell would not prevail against the offensive attacking spiritual forces that are taking ground in the hearts of our people.

God is not deterred by our failures. God is hurt and offended by our sin, but not daunted and his plan is not upended because of it. Details of the historical and biblical founding of the United

---

[191] Reagan, Ronald. Remarks at the Annual Convention of the the National Association of Evangelicals, 8 March 1983, Orlando, Florida.

States of America only serve to bolster this point. Other authors are more qualified in philosophical apologetics such as William Lane Craig[192] and Alvin Plantinga argue for the faith.[193] Plantinga makes the case that the proper place of religion and Christianity in our public life is needed. The religious affiliation of Presidents since George Washington (1732-1799) is overwhelmingly Christian. We embark on a journey to understand the role of religion in public life more broadly and help you answer the following questions. How do American Christians function as God-oriented people? What is the role of faith in the public square? How does the Church inform the practice of public service, formation, enforcement of laws, and shape our culture?

This book is not a polemic for electing only Christian politicians, but a recognition of how important the Christian faith is to our political life. Jimmy Carter (b. 1924) was a Christian and a poor president. Ronald Reagan was decidedly Christian but was private about his faith and mixed his belief system with secular influences. George H.W. Bush (1924-2018) and George W. Bush (b. 1946) shared a mainline Methodist upbringing that hardly tethered their global ambitions. Bill Clinton (b. 1946) was raised Baptist but was certainly the most secular president in our lifetime, before the election of the real-estate tycoon Donald Trump (b. 1946). Barack Obama (b. 1961) attended the Trinity United Church of Christ in Chicago under the pastorship of Rev. Jeremiah Wright (b. 1941) who taught Black liberation theology and Obama was likely influenced by his grandfather's

---

[192] Craig, W. L. (2000). The Kalam Cosmological Argument. United Kingdom: Wipf and Stock Publishers.
[193] Baker, Deane-Parker ed. (2007). Alvin Plantinga. United States: Cambridge University Press.

Muslim religion.[194] As Donald Trump entered office in 2016, he was a nominal Christian with a highly checkered past, accompanied by Mike Pence (b. 1959) his Vice-President and token evangelical. After his improbable election, he arguably did more to support religious freedom than his predecessors.

Being Christian is not a prerequisite for holding office. But Christianity must have its place at the head of the table for our country to function well. The church needs to be a part of every discussion in this country and guide our decisions toward godly morality and justice. We must have men and women of faith leading our nation because religion is a part of who we are. Our church should be honored and respected. And our faith, essential to who we are, must not be banned or outlawed. If that happens, and we turn our backs on God, we invite His wrath against us.

---

[194] Obama, B. (2007). Dreams from My Father: A Story of Race and Inheritance. United Kingdom: Crown.

8

Deified Leaders

RELIGION IS ONE of the organizing principles of a society. Religion alongside economy, culture, and language are the pillars of civilization. Assuming that the truth of religion can be assessed through the propositional claims that are made within it and arguments for the logical consistency and historical evidence of these claims, one religion stands out among all others. Christianity is demonstrably true in terms of its history, theory, and practice. The religion of Jesus Christ is the most scrutinized, widely disseminated, and most complete version of corporate worship of God across the planet. Christianity was spread throughout the world by the church which was led by men and women who preached a gospel of truth and spiritual freedom leading to political liberty. "So, Jesus said to the Jews who had believed him, 'If you abide in my word, you are truly my disciples, and you will know the truth, and the truth will set you free'" (John 8:31-32). The impact of Christianity on Western Civilization is profound, especially when compared to that of the influence of other religions on the modern world.

Leaders create, manage, and change culture; likewise, culture defines leadership for a group of people.[195] This dynamic has existed throughout history and the interaction between religion and leadership has shaped nations. This chapter will examine

---

[195] Schein, E. H., Schein, P. (2016). Organizational Culture and Leadership. Germany: Wiley.

the roots of religion and the way that faith affects society. Menes, Sargon, and Nimrod built empires around their power. Abraham was the father not only of the Jewish nation but the Christian church. Jesus is the paradigm of servant leadership and claimed his kingdom was spiritual and not physical. Paul spread the gospel through his witness and logical arguments. Then, Constantine rebuilt the Roman empire with religious devotion at the center of this renewal. Saint Augustine, one of the most influential Christian scholars, rejected false teachings and affirmed the supremacy of scripture. This progression over time of leaders influencing rather than coercing shows the direction of Christianity. Drawing a distinction between the example of Jesus and that of modern religious governments is found in *The Lincoln Legacy.*

The Foundations of Faith

Jesus founded the church by teaching His disciples to follow the message of His Kingdom and share the gospel of His salvation. When Jesus asked his followers, "Whom do people say the Son of Man is?" Simon Peter answered, "You are the Christ, the Son of the living God." Jesus replied, "Blessed are you, Simon son of Jonah! For this was not revealed to you by flesh and blood, but by My Father in heaven. And I tell you that you are Peter, and on this rock I will build My church, and the gates of Hades will not prevail against it" (Matthew 16:13b, 16-18). Jesus' declaration of his intent to establish His church through the leadership of the men he had trained was done to take spiritual ground from the Devil in the souls of humans. The goal of Jesus was to storm the gates of hell and release people from slavery to evil over the coming centuries. Throughout history kingdoms of this world have done battle, empires have risen and fallen, yet the church has persisted. Religion motivated the Thirty Years War and Islamic conquest,[196] but God has moved nations and armies across the world to accomplish his goals.

The church and state have been linked since the beginning of time and recorded history. Prophets, priests, and kings served various spiritual, judicial, and executive functions. Western Civilization uses documents to demarcate certain roles and positions. Like the US Constitution for America, in ancient Israel "the Deuteronomic Torah establishes itself as sole sovereign authority", redefining and limiting the role of the King concerning the other offices, both formal and informal, of prophet and priest, in the government.[197] *The Columbus Initiative* shows how the founding fathers of the US used this tradition which stems from English law, Enlightenment philosophy, and colonial charters, as a guide for the format of government in the US Constitution.[198] As discussed previously, once human beings could organize into cities there was a need for leaders to define our relationship to God or set up false gods among creation. Men did so to claim some special privilege or power. Mankind's rise from the Garden of Eden (exact location unknown), through the cradles of civilization in Africa, Egypt, Asia, and Ur, Mesopotamia, or modern-day Iraq included many religious practices.

---

[196] The European Wars of Religion: An Interdisciplinary Reassessment of Sources, Interpretations, and Myths. (2016). United Kingdom: Taylor & Francis.

[197] Levinson, B. (2001). The reconceptualization of kingship in Deuteronomy and the Deuteronomistic history's transformation of torah. Vetus Testamentum, 51(4), 511-534.

[198] Vile, M. J. C. (2012). Constitutionalism and the Separation of Powers. Liberty Fund.

Early Religion

In c. 3200 BC, King Menes (also called Narmer) of Egypt unified tribes into a kingdom that built a massive series of pyramids with hieroglyphs describing their worship of the pharaoh with Horus as a god-king in the line of gods.[199] Various "town gods" were worshiped in the ancient Middle East city-states before 2000 BC and until the rise of the Christian state.[200] "Polytheism is simply a less polemical substitute for what monotheistic traditions formerly called 'idolatry' and 'paganism' (Hebrew: *Zara*, Arabic: *shirk* or *jahiliya*)."[201] All religions make claims of acceptable and unacceptable beliefs. Judaism began around c. 1800 BC[202] when Abraham, a descendent of Noah, moved from Ur to Canaan based on his covenant with the singular deity that became known as Yahweh.[203] Zoroastrianism (1000 BC) was the Persian state religion for nearly one thousand years. Founded by Zoroaster (Zarathustra), it is dualistic (making distinctions between equal good and evil powers) and more polytheistic (multiple deities or demigods) than monotheistic. In this religion, Ahura Mazda (wisdom) is the supreme being, bringing Asha (order) out of one of the seven minor

---

[199] Shaw, Ian, ed. (2003). The Oxford History of Ancient Egypt. Oxford: Oxford University Press. p. 69. ISBN 0-19-280458-8.

[200] Peterson, E. (2011). Monotheism as a political problem: A contribution to the history of political theology in the Roman Empire. Theological tractates, 68-105.

[201] Assmann, J. (2004). Monotheism and polytheism. Religions of the Ancient World: A guide, 17-31.

[202] Dever, William G. (2002). What Did the Biblical Writers Know, and when Did They Know It?: What Archaeology Can Tell Us about the Reality of Ancient Israel. Wm. B. Eerdmans Publishing. ISBN 978-0-8028-2126-3.

[203] Mendes-Flohr, Paul (2005). "Judaism". In Thomas Riggs (ed.). Worldmark Encyclopedia of Religious Practices. 1. Farmington Hills, MI: Thomson Gale

deities, Spenta Mainyu (creativity), against Druj (falsehood and chaos) who came from Angra Mainyu (destruction).

Ancient Egypt is perhaps the oldest recorded civilization. It was based on a highly religious system of laws and beliefs. As a theocratic monarchy, the pharaoh was a God-king, a human representation of the divine.[204] He claimed that he was given to the people by the gods to guide and direct their lives. His job was to translate the will of the gods from the supernatural realm into action in the earthly kingdom. There was no debate or questioning his commands, issuing as if from the mouth of God. This mandate was always implied by birth and enforced by arms through the government structure and court advisers.

In 3150 BC, Narmer unified the country of Egypt into a single entity. Before that period, tribes were scattered in the Nile River basin and wars took place between the kingdoms of "Upper Egypt" and "Lower Egypt."[205] Some versions of government existed during The Scorpion Kings era of the Predynastic Period. However, exactly how this early form of tribal or warlord rule functioned is not known. We may assume that Egyptian religious beliefs have roots in this timeframe and the progression of religion follows the consolidation of power by Narmer.

What we see is that government draws from religious imagery. One explanation for this is that men used religion to manipulate people into accepting their reign. Early worship could be simply a primitive version of *The Wizard of Oz*. The king hides behind a curtain of supernatural threats to protect himself and his legacy. If claims that magic and technology could be controlled through stories about invisible deities who

---

[204] Levi, M. A. (1966). Political power in the ancient world. New American Library.
[205] https://www.ancient.eu/Egyptian_Government/

capriciously determined every aspect of life, from the rising and setting of the sun to growing seasons, wars, and even a mother's womb, then one person could perpetuate their influence and secure their place in the afterlife. Catacombs and temples filled with wealth is an ancient version of the bumper sticker adage "he who dies with the most toys wins."

This is a highly materialistic and modern interpretation of rites and systems that existed for thousands of years. Certain beliefs, such as an afterlife, are hardwired into us. We have very little evidence for how most people lived and worked in these countries before the modern era. Even up to the early eighteenth century very little documentary evidence has been collected about the notably harsh lives of peasants apart from their wages since the advent of written language estimated around 3000 BC.[206] Often the Great Man Theory of Leadership is reinforced because those are the only people of which we have records.[207] Religion seems to be a common thread across cultures, and every religion is defined in the relationship between the king and God. Yahweh is referred to as King of kings and Lord of lords.[208] The progression of thought between the Kingdom of Israel and the Kingdom of God demonstrates that mankind has sought to use the authority of God and misappropriate it for their power and purpose.[209] Monotheism induces conflict between the more parochial polytheistic religions of the ancient era and the

---

[206] Harris, R. (1986). The origin of writing (p. 29). London: Duckworth.
[207] Darnell, J. C. (2020). Origins of Writing in Northeastern Africa. In Oxford Research Encyclopedia of African History.
[208] Haring, J. W. (2017). "The Lord Your God is God of Gods and Lord of Lords": Is Monotheism a Political Problem in the Hebrew Bible?. political theology, 18(6), 512-527.
[209] Barker, M. (1992). The great angel: A study of Israel's second God. Westminster John Knox Press.

universal claims of an overarching vision for the union of spiritual and physical life.[210]

A Geographic Basis of Monotheism

Foundational ideas of religion originate in the creation mythology of the Bible and the *Epic of Gilgamesh*. These accounts have some similarities but differ significantly in their attempt to describe the origin of the cosmos. *Gilgamesh* does not include a flood story, that was added from the ancient Mesopotamian epic poem called *Atrahasis*.[211] Many cultures describe a worldwide flood like the story of Noah, including an Incan story where Andean farmers and llamas are preserved from the coming deluge in the mountain highlands.[212] The thread between religions is the sense of the divine and creation, both in the cosmos and in ourselves. Genesis includes the biblical account of creation echoed in Christianity and Islam, "In the beginning, God created the heavens and the earth. The earth was without form and void, and darkness was over the face of the deep. And the Spirit of God was hovering over the face of the waters" (Genesis 1:1-2). These ancient events include themes such as order versus chaos as well as redemption and judgment that are used to help us make sense of universal ideas.

Biblical references for the kingdom of Nimrod include the city of Akkad in the region of Sumer.[213] This overlap between

---

[210] Peterson, E. (2011). Monotheism as a political problem: A contribution to the history of political theology in the Roman Empire. Theological tractates, 68-105.

[211] Frymer-Kensky, T. (1977). The Atrahasis Epic and its Significance for Our Understanding of Genesis 1-9. The Biblical Archaeologist, 40(4), 147-155.

[212] Steele, P. R., & Allen, C. J. (2004). Handbook of Inca mythology. abc-clio.

[213] Walton, J. H., Carpenter, E. E., Wells, B., Cole, R. D., & Gane, R. (2009). Genesis, Exodus, Leviticus, Numbers, Deuteronomy (Vol. 1). Zondervan.

archaeological and Biblical locations supports the rise of kings. "He was the first on earth to be a mighty man. He was a mighty hunter before the Lord. Therefore, it is said, 'Like Nimrod a mighty hunter before the Lord'" (Genesis 10:8b-9). The dynasty of *Etana Kish* was created by an early king who was later celebrated in poems. Like the deluge myth, the ancient creation story titled *Enūma Eliš* was found on later Babylonian *Sumero-Akkadian* cuneiform tablets.[214] These portray a sexualized, graphic, and brutal god *Marduk* who tears the god *Tiamat* to pieces and uses her body to create the cosmos.[215] These stories are similar in form to those about *Gilgamesh*, king of the region called *Uruk*, who took control around 2700 BC.[216] *The Epic of Gilgamesh* dramatized his reign based on a creation myth that provided the origin story of all mankind. This was a way of connecting the exploits of humans to the providence of a god. It gives us a picture of an early leader whose position was based on his skill and guile.

According to Benson, "the Arabic has it, He was a terrible giant before the Lord: and the Syriac, He was a great warrior."[217] This commentary indicates that Nimrod led early group efforts to cultivate, use resources, and overpower others. On his relationship with his tribe, "It is probable he began with hunting… then he got to be their prince." He continues, "Great conquerors are but great hunters before the Lord. Alexander and Caesar would not make such a figure in Scripture history as they do in

---

[214] Budge, Wallis E.A. (1921). The Babylonian Legends of the Creation and the Fight between Bel and the Dragon. British Museum.

[215] Bryson, M. (2004). The Tyranny of Heaven: Milton's Rejection of God as King. United Kingdom: University of Delaware Press.

[216] Kramer, S. N. (1972). Sumerian mythology (Vol. 47). University of Pennsylvania Press.

[217] Benson, J. (1875). Commentary of the Old and New Testaments.

common history" because their accomplishments were through war. Many men have conquered and subdued other people. This is the "patriarchy" in our past, not a litany of all men but of some few conquerors who abused their power.

As Nimrod and Sargon claimed slaves for themselves, so have many kings. Sargon of Akkad (2340 BC) was the first king of the Akkadian Empire, named after his dynasty.[218] His conquest of Sumerian city-states formed one of the earliest recorded empires, a collection of kingdoms. The story of his birth is embellished in myth to make his reign appear destined by the gods. An ancient inscription reads, "My mother was a high priestess, my father I knew not. The brothers of my father loved the hills. My city is Azupiranu, which is situated on the banks of the Euphrates. My high priestess mother conceived me; in secret, she bore me. She set me in a basket of rushes, with bitumen she sealed my lid. She cast me into the river which rose over me. The river bore me up and carried me to Akki, the drawer of water. Akki, the drawer of water, took me as his son and reared me. Akki, the drawer of water, appointed me as his gardener. While I was a gardener, Ishtar granted me her love, and... I exercised kingship."[219] This story has an odd similarity to that of Moses being drawn out of the Nile River. Naturally, like Egyptian pharaohs, Babylonian kings wanted to claim the mantle of God for themselves. This privileged position of Great Men and now Great Women continue in spirit, if not the letter, of many modern organizations. Christianity provides a new model in Servant Leadership.[220]

---

[218] Oppenheim, A. L. (2013). Ancient Mesopotamia: portrait of a dead civilization. University of Chicago Press.

[219] Joan Goodnick Westenholz, Legends of the Kings of Akkade: The Texts (1997), 33–49.

[220] Niewold, J. (2007). Beyond servant leadership. Journal of Biblical Perspectives in Leadership, 1(2), 118-134.

Sumerian religion was polytheistic. Its culture was subsumed by Babylon in 2004 BC. Religious artifacts from the era of the *Epic of Gilgamesh* were not preserved, but a version of the text was edited by Sin-liqe-unninni (1200 BC).[221] Likewise, The Upanishads, Vedic religious texts of Hinduism describe a polytheistic series of gods. These documents are estimated to be composed between 700-600 BC, while some claim a date between 1000-1900 BC.[222,223] The earliest extant copy of the Vedas manuscript, the Rigveda and Atharvaveda, are dated to 1300 AD.[224] They contain the earliest emergence of central religious concepts of Hinduism, Buddhism, and Jainism. In contrast, the earliest biblical manuscripts, including the Old Testament or Torah, are dated to 150 BC to 70 AD, when most of the New Testament had been written.[225] The earliest nine parchment folios of the Quran are part of the Mingana collection held at the University Library of Birmingham and dated to the Seventh Century within decades of their origin.[226]

---

[221] Gertoux, G. (2015). Noah and the Deluge: Chronological, Historical and Archaeological Evidence. Lulu. com.

[222] The thirteen principal Upanishads: Translated from the Sanskrit with an outline of the philosophy of the Upanishads and an annotated bibliography. H. Milford, Oxford University Press, 1921.

[223] Edwin F. Bryant (2015). The Yoga Sutras of Patañjali: A New Edition, Translation, and Commentary. Farrar, Straus and Giroux. pp. 565–566. ISBN 978-1-4299-9598-6.

[224] Thapar, R. (2004). Early India: From the Origins to AD 1300. United States: University of California Press.

[225] Bruce, F. F. (1964). "The Last Thirty Years". In Frederic G. Kenyon (ed.). Story of the Bible.

[226] Fedeli, A. (2011). The provenance of the manuscript Mingana Islamic Arabic 1572: dispersed folios from a few Qur'anic quires. Manuscripta Orientalia. International Journal for Oriental Manuscript Research, 17(1), 45-56.

As the basis of many polytheistic or pantheistic religions, the Vedic texts oddly reference a single deity, Isa, who has been reinterpreted as the ground of being or some form of a creator. In many cases, pantheistic religions followed today are honored both as a source of wisdom and a way to convene with the spiritual realm by practitioners when asking for success or dealing with misfortune.[227] The Hindu holiday *Diwali* makes supplication to Lakshmi, the goddess of prosperity, prompting a celebration of the "victory of light over darkness, good over evil, and knowledge over ignorance."[228] This same model of unified contrast and dichotomy is found in Manicheism, a Persian version of Christianity, and many modern eastern religions. And while Christianity uses language comparing light and darkness (see: John 1:5; John 8:12; Ephesians 5:8; and Isaiah 9:2), it has documentation that within a generation of Jesus Christ's life and death people attested to his profound teaching, miracles, and claims.[229]

Judaism as a Bridge to Christianity

Judaism as a religion and the Hebrew form of governance started in the Babylonian plains. Abraham followed the norms of his age in Ur, a city of minor chieftains, family, and tribal possession of land, livestock, and people defining power within a polytheistic frame. However, after an encounter with the one true God, he was motivated by a desire for proper worship that required faithful obedience and rejected the false religion of his

---

[227] Kelly, J. D. (1988). From Holi to Diwali in Fiji: An essay on ritual and history. Man, 40-55.

[228] Jean Mead, How and why Do Hindus Celebrate Divali

[229] Yamauchi, E. M. (2003). Pre-Christian Gnosticism: a survey of the proposed evidences. Wipf and Stock Publishers.

family.[230] The status of many servants was indentured, some slaves were kept, others became like members of the family. Abraham was going to pass on his possessions to his most trusted employee, "O Lord God, what will you give me, for I continue childless, and the heir of my house is Eliezer of Damascus?" (Genesis 15:2). But God provided an heir in the person of Isaac, whose line continued through Jacob and his twelve sons, one of which, Joseph became the vizier, Prime Minister, likely to Pharaoh Amenemhat III of Egypt.[231]

An epic battle would ensue between false gods and Yahweh, the Great I AM, the God of Abraham, Isaac, and Jacob. God won and proved that man-made governments based on false claims of divinity are not theocratic but despotic. For nearly 400 years the Hebrew people had been slaves, then Moses led the Exodus of between three hundred thousand and over one million Jewish slaves from Egypt to the promised land of Canaan.[232] God told Abraham that the occupants of Canaan were wicked, and his descendants would take the land, "And they shall come back here in the fourth generation, the iniquity of the Amorites is not yet complete" (Genesis 15:16b). Amorites were the strongest tribe of the Canaanites whose cultic, pagan, and polytheistic practices, including necromantic witchcraft, violence, child sacrifice, and sex slavery were barbarous.[233] The people of Israel said to Joshua, "The Lord your God had commanded his servant Moses to give you all the land and to destroy all the inhabitants of the land"

---

[230] Armstrong, K. (1999). A history of God: From Abraham to the present: The 4000-year quest for God. Random House.

[231] Aling, C. F. (2020). Egypt and bible history: from earliest times to 1000 BC. Wipf and Stock Publishers.

[232] Rohl, D. M. (1995). Pharaohs and kings: A biblical quest. Crown.

[233] Unger, M. F. (1954). Archeology and the Old Testament. United Kingdom: Zondervan Publishing House.

(Joshua 9:24b). This was not a monstrous genocide as some claim.[234,235] While Israel was ordered to destroy all members of the tribes, Hebrew soldiers did not pursue those who fled. It was justified conquest, found in Exodus 23:23, Leviticus 18, Deuteronomy 7:1-2, and Joshua 3:10.

This progression from polytheistic religions to monotheism culminates in the Hebrew Exodus and conquest of Palestine. The only sustained attempt at a direct theocracy was ancient Israel. The nation was born through the lineage of Abraham (~2038 BCE).[236] Ancient Israel is often called a theocracy, but the period of direct guidance by God was limited to the Exodus and wandering in the wilderness which took place 400 years after the family of Jacob (also named Israel) moved to Egypt (in Genesis). After forty nomadic years, Israel engaged in a military invasion to take the promised land (in Exodus, Leviticus, Numbers, Deuteronomy). The visionary leadership of Moses gave way to the military leadership of Joshua. This led to a period of judges and prophets including Elijah and Elisha (see: Kings 1 and 2). As priestly leadership collapsed, God transformed the nation into a religious monarchy which fell into dynastic in-fighting and civil war for hundreds of years.

Over the next 1000 years, the tribe of Abraham grew into a nation, was dispersed, and returned to the promised land. King Saul, the first king of Israel, was replaced by David, God's anointed king, who was once a lowly shepherd boy and became a warrior and leader. His dynasty persisted within the

---

[234] Dawkins, R. (2011). The God Delusion. United Kingdom: Houghton Mifflin Harcourt.
[235] Hitchens, C. (2007). God Is Not Great: How Religion Poisons Everything. United Kingdom: Grand Central Publishing.
[236] Gertoux, G. (2017). Absolute chronology of Exodus.

divided kingdom after a civil war until the exile of Judah, the southern kingdom of Israel to Babylon. Upon the return of Jews to Jerusalem (see: Ezra, Nehemiah, and many of the minor prophets) and during the intertestamental period (between the record of the Old and New Testaments) Greek and Roman armies occupied the nation. But, even under puppet kings, eventually, the line of David was restored through Mary and Joseph in Jesus. Rather than throwing off the yoke of slavery only for the Jewish people, Jesus' Kingdom of God became the Christian church, and spread freedom throughout the world.

9

Christian Government
and Theology

HOW DID JESUS relate to the government of his day?

He paid taxes, when he was asked by the Pharisees, "Is it lawful to pay taxes to Caesar or not? Should we pay them or not?" But Jesus saw through their hypocrisy and said, "Why are you testing Me? Bring Me a denarius to inspect." So, they brought it, and He asked them, "Whose image is this? And whose inscription?" "Caesar's," they answered. Then Jesus told them, "Give to Caesar what is Caesar's, and to God what is God's." And they marveled at Him (Mark 12: 14b-17). Taxing power was enforced by the Roman garrison at Jerusalem which appointed helot leaders from subjugated tribes to rule over the Jewish people controlled by a religious class of priests and judges. And while Jesus viciously attacked the religious leaders of the day, he continued to observe the meaning behind the traditions they promoted. "Do not think that I have come to abolish the Law or the Prophets; I have not come to abolish them but to fulfill them" (Matthew 5:17). Jesus demonstrated respect for the civil authority, Edomite stewards in Herod's house, and Roman governors like Pilot. He never stirred up rebellion.[237]

Instead, Jesus challenged Pilot, "You would have no authority over me at all unless it had been given you from above. Therefore,

---

[237] Jensen, M. H. (2010). Herod Antipas in Galilee: The Literary and Archaeological Sources on the Reign of Herod Antipas and Its Socio-economic Impact on Galilee. Germany: Mohr Siebeck.

he who delivered me over to you has the greater sin" (John 19:11). Jesus' purpose was not to overthrow these unjust powers, but instead use them to accomplish his greater purpose. "Just as the Son of man came, not to be served to, but to serve, and to give his life as a ransom in exchange for many" (Matthew 20:28). Postmodernism decreases the overall respect for authority in a society but increases the demand for participative democracy.[238] However, Jesus put authority in its proper context even within a brutal military dictatorship. He respected leaders with whom he disagreed.

Jesus did not specifically provide recommendations for civil government, but his gospel and the church has led to the liberation of many people across the world of various stations, positions, races, and gender through the expansion of Christianity.[239] A record of this progress is detailed in sociological work on Christianity by Dennis,[240] LaTourette,[241] and Schmitt.[242] One recent acknowledgement is a useful example of even an atheist's willingness to accede to the transformational power of Christianity and the centrality of worldviews. Matthew Parris, a homosexual, atheist, and writer for the British Times, unknowingly commended Christianity's influence when he wrote, "Those who want Africa to walk tall amid 21st-century global

---

[238] Inglehart, R. (1999). Postmodernization erodes respect for authority, but increases support for democracy. Critical citizens: Global support for democratic government, 236-256.

[239] Bediako, K. (2004). Jesus And The Gospel In Africa: History And Experience (Theology in Africa Series). United Kingdom: Orbis Books.

[240] Dennis, J. S. (1898). Social Evils of the Non-Christian World. United Kingdom: Student volunteer movement for foreign missions.

[241] Latourette, K. S., & Winter, R. D. (1975). A history of Christianity (Vol. 2). New York: Harper & Row.

[242] Schmidt, A. J. (2004). How Christianity Changed the World. United States: Zondervan.

competition must not kid themselves that providing the material means or even the knowhow that accompanies what we call development will make the change. A whole belief system must first be supplanted."[243] This is the project of the church in Africa and across the globe.

Biblical theology and orthodox Christianity assert God's sovereignty over government. Regardless of how a leader is installed through conquest, coup, or elections, "The king's heart is in the hand of the Lord" (Proverbs 21:1a). It is helpful to view Jesus' relationship with the government that would execute him in the context of his life and teaching ministry. Jesus knew that his cousin, John the Baptist, would suffer for his prophetic acts. John was often compared to Elijah the Prophet. Jesus said, "I tell you, among those born of women no one is greater than John. Yet the one who is least in the kingdom of God is greater than he is" (Luke 7:17). In many ways, Jesus left it to him to directly challenge the power structure of his day. John the Baptist confronted Herod Antipas about his scandalous affair with his brother's ex-wife and was beheaded unjustly because of this.[244] Therefore, Jesus allowed and even encouraged verbal confrontations with political leaders.

Similarly, Jewish temple practices were legally sanctioned by the Roman government to placate the population. Roman laws allowed worship of local gods so long as this did not compete with a reverence for Caesar's divinity. But Jesus rejected the Hebrew compromise, "And making a whip of cords, he drove them all out of the temple, with the sheep and oxen. And he poured out

---

[243] http://www.timesonline.co.uk/tol/comment/columnists/matthew_parris/article5400568.ece

[244] Scobie, C. H. (1961). John the Baptist (Doctoral dissertation, ProQuest Dissertations & Theses,).

the coins of the money-changers and overturned their tables" (John 2:15). Jesus was under no delusion about the corruption and avarice of these pseudo-leaders of the Sanhedrin, the judicial governing body of Jewish religious leaders. Toxic, destructive, or pseudo leadership exercises coercive and deceptive power to elevate themselves and accomplish their own personal agenda.[245] In many ways, based on our human assessments, the good done by the best leaders is outweighed by all the bad done by the worst leaders through history and organizations. Thus, preventing the corrupting influence of bad leadership is more important than transformational changes.

But God can use even the vilest people as instruments to accomplish His good in the midst of suffering. As an example, Joseph challenged his brothers who nearly killed him and instead sold him into slavery to appease their own guilt. "As for you, you meant evil against me, but God meant it for good, to bring it about that many people should be kept alive, as they are today" (Genesis 50:20). God can use what was meant for evil to accomplish his good. "And we know that for those who love God all things work together for good, for those who are called according to his purpose" (Romans 8:28). Throughout history the church has adapted to social conventions without compromise, worked to alleviate cultural rot, and found ways around government systems to bring redemption to many people.

Our understanding of religion in modern America is shaped by our Christian background and the philosophical, sociological, and legal structures that define common discourse. Critical thinking requires the ability to consider the flaws and limitations

---

[245] Krasikova, D. V., Green, S. G., & LeBreton, J. M. (2013). Destructive leadership: A theoretical review, integration, and future research agenda. Journal of management, 39(5), 1308-1338.

of any system of thinking or mental models.[246] Many leaders who abuse their position have claimed to represent religious powers or transformational change. A pseudo-transformational leader is characterized by unethical practices that at a minimum violate the followership and freedom of those depending on them and at a maximum conduct illegal activity.[247] Biases inherent in these toxic forms of leadership are instructive in our assessment of how prototypes, leniency, and general satisfaction of followers can endorse these manipulators.[248] Concurrently, leaders who take advantage of situational factors may benefit from halo effects where one positive attribute becomes a proxy for a constellation of characteristics that they do not possess.[249] However, there are certain leaders who rise to the challenge, survive the crucible and become a guidepost for future generations.

Throughout this book claims are made that weave together biblical, philosophical, and logical positions. The goal is to be consistent in the application of principles while allowing for the faults and failures of human beings. We are not perfect, and therefore God must use broken vessels to accomplish His purposes. But rest assured, His plan will be secured. There are practical and political positions that many people disagree on.

---

[246] Halpern, D. F. (1998). Teaching critical thinking for transfer across domains: Disposition, skills, structure training, and metacognitive monitoring. American psychologist, 53(4), 449.

[247] Barling, J., Christie, A., & Turner, N. (2008). Pseudo-transformational leadership: Towards the development and test of a model. Journal of Business Ethics, 81(4), 851-861.

[248] Bass, B. M., & Avolio, B. J. (1989). Potential biases in leadership measures: How prototypes, leniency, and general satisfaction relate to ratings and rankings of transformational and transactional leadership constructs. Educational and psychological measurement, 49(3), 509-527.

[249] Lievens Pascal Van Geit Pol Coetsier, F. (1997). Identification of transformational leadership qualities: An examination of potential biases. European Journal of Work and Organizational Psychology, 6(4), 415-430.

However, disagreements on these points need not devolve into a theological debate. There are many arguments which, taken on face value, should garner widespread support based on reason alone. Doctrines in Mere or Classic Christianity provide the widest truthful interpretation of orthodoxy that can encompass the Church. While many people who claim to know and follow Jesus are liars, we will leave that to God to sort out. Unambiguous sins which are clear and known should be called out. The contours of the faith here are painted with broad strokes. In rare cases, specific theological positions are taken and noted.

Policing Doctrinal Issues

Many philosophies or teachings such as Arianism and Manichaeism are examples of heresy that have resurfaced throughout the history of the Christian church. The popular author and professor Jordan Peterson adapted his own version of this dualistic teaching of chaos and order through his Jungian archetypal psychology which he used in his various books and lectures to spark conversations about the transcendent and eternal.[250] These ideas are compelling and appealing because they explain our intuitions about the world in terms of impersonal forces. But too often religion and ideology become tools of leaders to control and motivate people rather than the proper means to worship God. Peterson recognizes this tendency in his work on totalitarian regimes, but he views religion as a psychological construct rather than a more accurate description of the objective reality he acknowledges exists, preferring the idea of interpersonal subjectivity. All religions should be measured against

---

[250] Peterson, J. B. (1999). Maps of meaning: The architecture of belief. Psychology Press.

reality. Within systematic theology, religion has terminology to deal with deviations from the norm. Anything that strays from orthodoxy is heresy. However, the way that Christians have applied the definition of heresy and understand orthodoxy has varied throughout the centuries.[251]

A curious progression of thought took place from ancient Asia by way of Middle Eastern Judaism to Roman Catholic Christianity found in a dualistic heresy which was entertained and eventually rejected by St. Augustine of Hippo (354-400 AD). A Persian named Mani (c. 216–274) developed a cult based on Christianity merging elements of Zoroastrianism with biblical principles. In his teaching, light and darkness are at war and humanity are pawns or tools for the entertainment of these divine forces. Manichaeism is a polytheistic understanding of gods as capricious and arbitrary combined with the Christian teaching on God and Satan as oppositional beings of good and evil, respectively. Related ideas are in the Bible but only when put in their proper moral context will they help us understand our sin nature and God's holiness.

Paul admonished believers, "Do not be unequally yoked with unbelievers. For what partnership has righteousness with lawlessness? Or what fellowship has light with darkness?" (2 Corinthians 6:14). This parallel between light and darkness, like order and chaos, is found in Jesus' own words. Jesus said, "I am the light of the world. Whoever follows me will not walk in darkness but will have the light of life" (John 8:12). Earlier in the book of John, Jesus was compared to light, "In him was life, and the life was the light of men. The light shines in the darkness, and

---

[251] Russell, J. B. (1992). Dissent and Order in the Middle Ages: The Search for Legitimate Authority. United States: Wipf and Stock Publishers.

the darkness has not overcome it" (John 1:4-5). So, the idea of light and darkness, like the Chinese symbol of the yin-yang, can be helpful to understand contrasting ideas which are mutually exclusive. This is but one example of many thematic or symbolic elements in religious language. However, we should not understand the dark side as something to be trifled with or on par with God. Unlike Jedi Knights becoming Sith Lords, there are no acts of redemption to save us, such as throwing the emperor down the Death Star reactor shaft.[252] Instead we look to Jesus, "For everyone who calls on the name of the Lord will be saved" (Romans 10:13).

Dealing with Good and Evil

In Christianity, Satan is viewed as an extremely powerful and manipulative being. The name Satan is more of a title and simply means accuser.[253] Like Manichaeism, every heresy makes the mistake of either outright false teaching or, more likely, perverting truth with falsehoods such as taking a minor point and making it a major one. A partial truth can become a complete lie. Too often created beings, like the Devil, compare themselves to God, "You made the mistake and thought that I was just like you" (Psalm 50:21). Satan may be the evilest created being, but he is not the paradigm of evil the way that God is the source of goodness. God created Satan, "For thus says the Lord, who created the heavens, he is God! Who formed the earth and made it, he established it; he did not create it empty, he formed

---

[252] Schulets, John. (2003). Any Gods Out There? Perceptions of Religion from Star Wars and Star Trek. Journal of Religion & Film, 7(2), 3.

[253] Friedman, H. H., & Lipman, S. (1999). Satan the Accuser: Trickster in Talmudic and Midrashic Literature. Friedman, HH & Lipman, S.(1999). Satan the Accuser: Trickster in Talmudic and Midrashic Literature, Thalia: Studies in Literary Humor, 18, 31-41.

it to be inhabited: 'I am the Lord, and there is no other'" (Isaiah 45:18). And to the degree that he allows competition with Satan to exist it is limited for a time and purpose.

Jesus didn't consider the Devil to be his equal. During his temptation in the wilderness, he refused to bow before him even at the point of starvation, "Then Jesus said to him, 'Away with you, Satan! For it is written, "You shall worship the Lord your God, and Him only you shall serve"'" (Matthew 4:10). When he called out the Pharisees, this political religious sect in first century Israel, he made this link, "You belong to your father, the devil, and you want to carry out your father's desires. He was a murderer from the beginning, not holding to the truth, for there is no truth in him. When he lies, he speaks his native language, for he is a liar and the father of lies" (John 8:44). As St. Augustine entertained the dualistic ideas of two rival deities before rejecting this heresy, many people must work through false teaching to find the truth. He was educated in Carthage through Greek and Latin culture where he learned about Manichaeism.[254] He eventually rejected it and taught against this heresy, emphasizing a more Neoplatonist compatibilism which taught that evil was the absence or perversion of the good.[255]

Christianity has dealt with many philosophies which attempt to juxtapose God and the good. Rehashing the Euthyphro dilemma is necessary to better understand the arguments against God as the source of morality which can help distinguish the role of evil and good in our political systems. This mental exercise is in Plato's *Dialogues* where Socrates asks a series of questions that

---

[254] Pope, Hugh (1911). "St. Monica". In Herbermann, Charles (ed.). Catholic Encyclopedia. 10. New York: Robert Appleton Company.
[255] O'Donnell, James (2005). Augustine: A New Biography. New York, NY: HarperCollins. pp. 45, 48.

can be summarized, "is something good because it pleases the gods, or is it pleasing to the gods because it's good?"[256] William Lane Craig dispels this false dilemma by grounding morality in the character of God. "God wills something because he is good. That is to say it is God's own nature which determines what is good."[257] It is also possible to ground God's commands in his love for us, thus rejecting both horns of Socrates' mindbender.[258] Dealing with heresy starts with intellectual debates.

However, many modernists refuse to let this contention die and beat it to a pulp. Harari writes, "So, monotheism explains order, but is mystified by evil. Dualism explains evil but is puzzled by order. There is one logical way of solving the riddle: to argue that there is a single omnipotent God who created the entire universe—and He's evil. But nobody in history has had the stomach for such a belief."[259] Fredrich Nietzsche (1844-1900), a German anti-Christian philosopher, and his acolytes came very close to embracing this solution, spurring hatred for God. A more logical and consistent conclusion is preferred. If you believe the Euthyphro Dilemma is still a problem, this may entertain you personally but it leads to illogical thinking that can produce mistaken conclusions that have serious ramifications for individuals and society. If we refuse to accept God as the source and paradigm of goodness, we will pursue evil at our own pace. While questions are not heretical, they can lead to serious errors both inside and outside of the church. Christianity distinguishes between sin, missing the mark of moral acts, and heresy, false

---

[256] Plato. (2009). Four Dialogues: Wildside Press, LLC.
[257] Craig, W. L. (2010). On guard: Defending your faith with reason and precision. David C Cook.
[258] Macbeath, M. (1982). The euthyphro dilemma. Mind, 91(364), 565-571.
[259] Harari, Y. N. (2014). Sapiens: A brief history of humankind. Random House.

belief, or teaching, which are related to the concepts of *herem* (Judaism), devoted to destruction, and *haram* (Islam), that which is forbidden.[260] It is necessary to define various forms of heresy as a way of understanding how the church must monitor errors.

The Problem with Heresy

Heresies are false doctrines taught as truth. The Arian heresy opposed by Constantine is one example. Arius (256–336) was an Antiochian church leader in Alexandria Egypt who taught against trinitarianism that God the Father and Jesus Christ were not God together, externally coexistent, and equal.[261] Early church fathers Tertullian and Irenaeus discussed the difference between the divine "economy" in the Trinity where interrelationships exist in the godhead and what can be called the ontology of the Trinity where the Father, Son, and Holy Spirit are three distinct persons in one God, as a title for the divine.[262] For example, "And when Jesus was baptized, immediately he went up from the water, and behold, the heavens were opened to him, and he saw the Spirit of God descending like a dove and coming to rest on him; and behold, a voice from heaven said, "This is my beloved Son, with whom I am well pleased" (Matthew 3:16–17). This theology expresses the truths of scripture in doctrine.

This was addressed at the Council of Nicaea in 325. Constantine exiled anyone who explicitly rejected the Nicean creed, including Arius, Euzoios, Libyan bishops Theonas of

---

[260] Hofreiter, C. (2018). Making Sense of Old Testament Genocide: Christian Interpretations of Herem Passages. United Kingdom: OUP Oxford.
[261] Rahner, K. (2001). The trinity. Bloomsbury Publishing.
[262] Gunton, C. (1990). Augustine, the Trinity and the Theological Crisis of the West1. Scottish Journal of Theology, 43(1), 33-58.

Marmarica, and Secundus of Ptolemais.[263] Constantine also ordered that the Thalia, Arius' book, be burned. Is it ever appropriate to limit ideas? Only when they are a clear threat to readers. Spreading lies under the freedom of press and speech are a modern dilemma and while we tend to provide a large degree of latitude, we must always revisit these issues. Paul clearly taught that false teachers would lead people astray. "See to it that no one takes you captive through hollow and deceptive philosophy, which depends on human tradition and the elemental spiritual forces of this world rather than on Christ" (Colossians 2:8). However, there are three categories of heretical teaching that should be addressed.

Pure heresy is teaching lies for the purpose of deception. It is like manipulation and propaganda because it claims a source of authority.[264] This is the effort of Satanic forces and evil people to attack God and His church. "But false prophets also arose among the people, just as there will be false teachers among you, who will secretly bring in destructive heresies, even denying the Master who bought them, bringing upon themselves swift destruction" (2 Peter 2:1). The manner of pure heresy may include the nature and character of God or his plan. This is the most clear and destructive form of heresy and leads to individual damnation.

Practical heresy is the set of unorthodox beliefs that harm individuals and groups that believe and spread them. "For if someone comes and proclaims another Jesus than the one, we proclaimed, or if you receive a different spirit from the one you received, or if you accept a different gospel from the one you

---

[263] Ayres, L. (2004). Nicaea and Its Legacy: An Approach to Fourth-Century Trinitarian Theology. United Kingdom: OUP Oxford.
[264] Bernays, E. L. (1928). Propaganda. United States: Ig Publishing.

accepted, you put up with it readily enough" (2 Corinthians 11:4). If you accept it and you put up with it readily enough you will suffer the consequences of corruption. "If anyone comes to you and does not bring this teaching, do not receive him into your house or give him any greeting" (2 John 1:10). Practical heresies are also called heterodoxy and tend to give rise to cults.

Preferential heresy is the basis of conflict in groups of believers. In many cases these are personal and controversial in nature. These errors are not in doctrine per se, they are about how we conduct ourselves in the body of Christ. "As for a person who stirs up division, after warning him once and then twice, have nothing more to do with him" (Titus 3:10). It must be noted that this brand of heresy cuts both ways, the accuser and the accused must be evaluated by the body of believers. It requires a form of legality, and the weight of evidence must be substantial. Church discipline is the broad category under which these disputes fall. You should not slander a brother or sister in the Lord because you disagree about the use of drums in a worship service or singing Psalms without music. But many do. However, sexual harassment and extramarital affairs do serious damage to a local body of believers and may compromise the public witness of a pastor and thus lead people astray. Attempting to cover for someone will damage the church. And personal self-interest must not be elevated above truth.

10

Christian Particularism

CHRISTIANITY IS A religion based on consent. Throughout the New Testament belief is emphasized as the key to unlocking the temporal and eternal benefits of a relationship with God. Jesus preached the forgiveness of sin, "The time is fulfilled, and the kingdom of God is at hand; repent and believe in the gospel" (Mark 1:15). No other religion addresses the individual as clearly and completely as Christianity. In forthcoming books, *The Columbus Initiative* and *The Lincoln Legacy* we will explore the expression of Christian freedom found in America.

Augustine's *Confessions* show the conversion of one man from heresy to a man that was used by God. It emphasized our innate conscience that is essential to biblical theology (ex. In Romans 2:15) as he shares his personal experience. He later wrote in the City of God to refute the claim that Christianity caused the fall of Rome, and instead made the argument that the church is instrumental in the ultimate success of the greater empire as part of the Kingdom of Heaven.[265] His reflections laid the foundation for future interactions between the church and state, laying out principles for a Just War theory and the rejection of secular rule. This leads us to ask, should we as Christians reflect the values of the society in which we live, or do we live counter-culturally? And if so, what counterculture do we represent? Certainly, a biblical worldview is different from the secular.

---

[265] Augustine. The City of God. (1903). United Kingdom: J. M. Dent.

This is the nature of religion. However, the Jewish culture of the Old Testament is not that of the first-century church or European denominations, let alone that of modern Christianity. The church should support American culture to the extent that it maintains Christian values. If that is no longer the case the church should oppose it.

Foundationally, every religion makes exclusive claims about reality, and these claims require scrutiny. Walter Martin (1928-1989) wrote, "Truth by definition is exclusive. If truth were all-inclusive, nothing would be false."[266] If Christianity is true for me, that means that it is true for you. We do not believe in gravity simply out of some personal preference. We take these ideas and principles and live them out. As Nancy Pearcey writes, "Having a Christian worldview means being utterly convinced that biblical principles are not only true but also work better in the grit and grime of the real world."[267] As Paul admonished us, "Do not be conformed to this world but be transformed by the renewal of your mind, that by testing you may discern what is the will of God, what is good and acceptable and perfect" (Romans 12:2). therefore we should challenge false claims. We must avoid the temptations and the "worries and riches and pleasures of this life" (Luke 8:14). We must search the Bible and continually apply *Berean* testing to anyone who claims Jesus as Lord. We should emulate the critical thinking of Berea, "they received the word with all readiness of mind, and searched the scriptures daily, whether those things were so" (Acts 17:11). False teachers such as Joel Osteen (b. 1963), Creflo Dollar (b. 1962), Kenneth Copeland (b. 1936) have attempted to pander to greed and play

---

[266] Martin, W. R. (1965). The Kingdom of Cults. Minneapolis: Bethany Fellowship.
[267] Pearcey, N. (2004). Total truth. Wheaton. Crossway.

off the needs of people shilling a false gospel and heresy. Jim Bakker (b. 1940), a televangelist, has been sued for selling a silver formula with claims that it will heal COVID-19.[268]

False teachers who engage in pure heresy fail to recognize the contradictions in their practices. They preach that sin is preventing your health, but rarely do they address sin in all other aspects of life. These men and women damage the overall witness of the church and reduce the effectiveness of Christian leaders. Instead of looking at politics as a policy, it is more accurate to define politics as the use of power. Christians who are political leaders must deal with many difficult and dirty topics. Politics plays out more like the courtiers of an ancient or medieval king than the talking heads on cable news stations. Unfortunately, office politics determine the success of various projects in a business. In the same way, interpersonal politics even at the national level will affect policy and thus the church's ability to shape our future. To further depict the ways that the church has succeeded or failed requires an accounting of failures and setbacks.

Christian leaders must reconcile the adage "if tribes or nations states fight over resources the victor is deemed right" which is often quoted as "history is written by the victors."[269] The truth will aid successful enterprises, but with success comes complacency and corruption. In practice, nations attempt to control the narrative of their society. This has become more insidious in the era of massive technology oligopolies. While

---

[268] See: https://www.npr.org/2020/03/11/814550474/missouri-sues-televangelist-jim-bakker-for-selling-fake-coronavirus-cure, and https://www.fda.gov/inspections-compliance-enforcement-and-criminal-investigations/press-releases/court-orders-halt-sale-silver-product-fraudulently-touted-covid-19-cure

[269] Histoire de la royauté: considérée dans ses origines, jusqu'à la formation des principales monarchies de l'Europe 1842.

we know that in the end, God will be victorious, we must fight for truth and justice today. Alexis de Tocqueville (1805-1859) commenting on the American civil society, church, and state considering the role of democracy, freedom, and religion wrote the following, "The short space of threescore years can never content the imagination of man; nor can the imperfect joys of this world satisfy his heart. Man alone, of all created beings, displays a natural contempt of existence, and yet a boundless desire to exist; he scorns life, but he dreads annihilation." We hunger for the eternal and live like we are dying. He goes on:

"These different feelings incessantly urge his soul to the contemplation of a future state, and religion directs his musings thither. Religion, then, is simply another form of hope, and it is no less natural to the human heart than hope itself. Men cannot abandon their religious faith without a kind of aberration of intellect and a sort of violent distortion of their true nature; they are invincibly brought back to more pious sentiments. Unbelief is an accident, and faith is the only permanent state of mankind.

If we consider religious institutions merely from a human point of view, they may be said to derive an inexhaustible element of strength from man himself, since they belong to one of the constituent principles of human nature. I am aware that at certain times religion may strengthen this influence, which originates in itself, by the artificial power of the laws and by the support of those temporal institutions that direct society. Religions intimately united with the governments of the earth have been known to exercise sovereign power founded on terror and faith; but when a religion contracts an alliance of this nature, I do not hesitate to affirm that it commits the same error as a man who should sacrifice his future to his present welfare; and in obtaining a power to which it has no claim, it risks that authority which is rightfully it is own.

When a religion founds its empire only upon the desire of immortality that lives in every human heart, it may aspire to universal dominion; but when it connects itself with a government, it must adopt maxims that apply only to certain nations. Thus, in allying with political power, religion augments its authority over a few and forfeits the hope of reigning over all.

As long as a religion rests only upon those sentiments which are the consolation of all affliction, it may attract the affections of all mankind. But if it is mixed up with the bitter passions of the world, it may be constrained to defend allies whom its interests, and not the principle of love, have given to it; or to repel as antagonists men who are still attached to it, however, opposed they may be to the powers with which it is allied. The church cannot share the temporal power of the state without being the object of a portion of that animosity which the latter excites."[270]

De Tocqueville beautifully explains the tension between government and the church that America's founders dealt with. He was fully aware of the ideology which motivated the French Revolution (1789-1799). With religious fervor, the blood of the

---

[270] Alexis de Tocqueville (1835), Democracy in America.

guillotine was spread, and the Temple of Reason was erected. De Tocqueville supported the Bourbons against the Second Empire and then Louis-Eugène Cavaignac (1802-1857) against the nephew of Napoléon, Louis Napoléon Bonaparte III (1808-1873). He had opposed a coup to reestablish a Bonapartist monarchy in 1851. He was held as a political prisoner at Vincennes and released. Eventually, he abandoned politics and retired at Château de Tocqueville where he eventually died because of tuberculosis at the age of fifty-four.

Compare the results of the French revolution in central controls, libertine freedoms, the use of violence, and unquestioned power with those of the American revolution. The American Revolution was tied to religious liberty, local government, self-governance, Constitutional law, civil society through mediating institutions, rights, freedoms, and fair elections. Without these conditions and principles, our revolution fails. But the French Revolution shared none of this restraint. During the French Reign of Terror, 17,000 people were executed, and during the Napoleonic wars 2.5 million military deaths are estimated and nearly 1 million civilians died.[271] During the American revolution there were 6,800 colonist military deaths, another 12,000-17,000 people were killed as prisoners of Great Britain and about 5,000 died from diseases.[272] Conversely, about 24,000 British soldiers were killed fighting Americans.[273] Consider the results of the Russian (1917-1921) Revolution led by Bolshevik Communists which established a dictatorship, starvation, poverty, and the use of a police state to report on, manipulate, and control the population. Between 20-30 million people died in

---

[271] https://www.history.com
[272] https://www.battlefields.org
[273] Ibid

Lenin's Great Terror and the Ukrainian Holodomor alone, and another 9 million are attributed to armed conflict with untold millions of unnatural deaths occurring elsewhere.[274] These three great political revolts took place within 150 years.

Jesus did not want to be an earthly king. So, we shouldn't expect him to rule over our nation today. However, he called leaders throughout history who honored him and fought for our freedom. The New Testament did not recommend that Christians should take over the Roman Empire, start the Protestant Reformation, or found America. But these actions are entirely in the purview of right and proper doctrine. God did not send a prophet to tell us the exact outcome of future generations of Christians. Instead, He provided a broad timeline in which we will act to bring about the Kingdom of God and the redemption of mankind. Some believers like Rod Dreher (b. 1967) think that now we should just hunker down and love our neighbor as ourselves. These holy huddles have never worked in the monasteries, ministries, or separatist communities of friends. They either devolve into cultic practices or atrophy because of their cannibalistic tendencies.

As we will see in *The Columbus Initiative*, the monastery failed to promote greater holiness in living within the culture, so too the throne room failed to capture land and lives for the gospel. However, both restraint and conviction produced the combination of freedom and order on which American ideals are based on. Making the case for *The Constantine Doctrine* requires debunking the lies about the purpose and foundation of America while accurately dealing with our faults and sins. Paul was strategic by not threatening the Roman Empire directly and

---

[274] https://www.heritage.org

unlike Islam never promoted conversion by the sword. Christ taught his disciples to change hearts and minds to reach the soul. The Prophets, Paul, and Jesus called out unjust systems and the sinfulness of men. Jesus warned, "Beware of false prophets, who come to you in sheep's clothing, but inwardly are ravenous wolves" (Matthew 7:15). Many people have used Christ to gain power. Like greedy politicians, false teachers push their agenda for control and wealth instead of sacrificially loving others and laying down their own lives. What would our country look like if more leaders emulated Jesus?

Kingdoms Under God

Kingdoms rise and fall. Empires are established. God reigns over all. He prophesied in Daniel in Chapters 2, 7, and 8 the procession of empires before Christ. God rejects our desire to overthrow governments in rebellion or revolution for personal gain. But he may use us to do so to advance freedom in the gospel. In the same way, as the Hebrew Kingdom and the Roman Empire became the vehicle for the transmission of the Christian gospel, America has been an agent of God in the modern era. This is different from a theocracy. It requires that a people worship God and continue to do so to retain His blessing.

In 333 BC, Medo-Persian rule over the Middle East ended when Darius III (381-330 BC) was defeated by Alexander the Great (356-323 BC). Alexander established the Greek Empire, which was broken into four kingdoms, the *Diadochi*, upon his death. Generals were the "successors" to Alexander and agreed to go their separate ways. Lysimachus (360 BC – 281 BC) claimed Thrace, Asia Minor, which is mostly modern-day Turkey. Cassander (355-297 BC) maintained local control of Macedonia and Greece as the seat of the Empire. Ptolemy I (367-283 BC) took over Egypt, Israel, Cilicia, Petra, and Cyprus. Seleucus I Nicator (358-281 BC) established the western edge of the empire which eventually spread to Jordan, Mesopotamia, Persia, and Northern India. To greater or lesser extents, these regions were Hellenized as Greek, and these philosophical, cultural, and religious beliefs influenced the people of the Middle East before the birth of Christ. The Greek Empire was assumed by the Roman Empire after the Battle of Corinth (146 BC); later the steward Herod Agrippa (11 BC – 44 AD) was installed, and Pontius Pilate (20? BC – 37 AD) governed Palestine. God established the church under this empire.

Instead of the ancient practice of merging leaders and gods, let us treat men as sinful and fallible. This will prevent us from making the mistakes of revering people so much that we allow them to assume power granted only to God. His authority is absolute. His law is just. We simply attempt to mirror God's holiness with righteous leadership as much as we are able. Often this quote from James Madison (1751-1836) is taken out of context and we must take the same liberty, "If men were angels, no government would be necessary. If angels were to govern men, neither external nor internal controls on government would be necessary."[275] But we sinful men must learn to lead well. David writes of God's view of man, "Yet you have made him a little lower than the angels and crowned him with glory and honor" (Psalm 8:5). While Madison is referring specifically to the need for checks and balances within the structure of government, like David, his observation serves to make the case for what Thomas Sowell (b. 1930) calls the constrained vision of human beings.[276]

---

[275] The Federalist No. 51, James Madison
[276] A Conflict of Visions: Ideological Origins of Political Struggles, by Thomas Sowell

He writes, "moral limitations of man in general, and his egocentricity in particular" must be treated as limitations on what we can accomplish on our own. This instills humility which is necessary to lead well.

Modern American Appeasement

All governments make laws based on ethics and morality. Our model for the relationship between Christians and government is most clearly outlined in Romans. Paul gave the Christian clear directions on their relationship to government and described the proper role of government in this world. He declared, "Let everyone be subject to the governing authorities, for there is no authority except that which God has established. The authorities that exist have been established by God." The key idea is that the government that governs best not only governs least but governs justly. "For rulers hold no terror for those who do right, but for those who do wrong. Do you want to be free from fear of the one in authority? Then do what is right and you will be commended. For the one in authority is God's servant for your good. But if you do wrong, be afraid, for rulers do not bear the sword for no reason. They are God's servants, agents of wrath to bring punishment on the wrongdoer." Good governors must not be corrupt. Leaders should condemn evil and recommend good conduct, or they will see more evil and less good.

We need good leaders, but we often must deal with unjust rulers. This topic is addressed more fully in the American Revolution. Paul goes on, "Consequently, whoever rebels against the authority is rebelling against what God has instituted, and those who do so will bring judgment on themselves. Therefore, it is necessary to submit to the authorities, not only because of possible punishment but also as a matter of conscience. This is also why you pay taxes, for the authorities are God's servants, who give their full time to governing. Give to everyone what you owe them: If you owe taxes, pay taxes; if revenue, then revenue; if respect, then respect; if honor, then honor" (Romans 13:1-7). Peter generalizes godly respect to include earthly kings, "Honor everyone. Love the brotherhood. Fear God. Honor the emperor" (1 Peter 2:17). We should support and defend the just laws of our nation which were founded without a king. The supreme law of the United States remains the Constitution as originally written and thus we honor God when we hold to our founding.

Because our laws are based on morality, some laws promote character but others ridicule righteous behavior because of sinful lawmakers. When people with overlapping and diverging interests interact in a bounded area there will be conflict. This requires wisdom to navigate the halls of power. When our discourse is rife with false claims it muddies the water of law and policy. Peter notes, "But there were also false prophets among the people, even as there will be false teachers among you, who will secretly bring in destructive heresies, even denying the Lord who bought them and bring on themselves swift destruction. And many will follow their destructive ways, because of whom the way of truth will be blasphemed. By covetousness they will exploit you with deceptive words; for a long time, their judgment has not been idle, and their destruction does not slumber" (2 Peter 2:1-3). False teaching is not limited to the church, it impacts our lives in many ways including our government.

We must be very aware of the dangers posed by people who misrepresent the Christian faith, even those who mistakenly fall into error for political purposes. The Constantine Doctrine is developed through this series with the idea that Christianity is the model religion. It incorporates the most important supernatural aspects of historical modes of worship of the divine and the rational or modern aspects of a scientific and philosophical worldview to draw logical inferences from moral teaching. Further, Christianity has policed its theology and rejected the perversion and distortion of truths found in many religious and ideological teachings across time and geography. In striving for justice, we must beat back the forces that darken the minds of our countrymen. All leaders should abide by the truth, "Whoever says 'I know him' but does not keep his commandments is a liar, and the truth is not in him, but whoever keeps his word, in him truly the love of God is perfected. By this we may know that we are in him: whoever says he abides in him ought to walk in the same way in which he walked" (1 John 2:4-6). And we must hold our leaders accountable whatever the cost.

The suspense has built long enough. Next, we turn to the man Constantine himself. We peel back layers of history to better understand his own life and grasp his motivations. What is his legacy as a leader, a Christian, and a man? Regardless of how he understood himself, how he was understood by his contemporaries, or how he is represented in history; God had a plan for this Roman soldier of fortune. He was protected from numerous disasters, and saw victories which rather than attached to fate, he attributed to God's hand.

11

The First Christian Head of State

CONSTANTINE (273-337 AD) is one of the most celebrated and misunderstood men of history generally and in Christianity specifically. His accomplishments are many, yet his motivation and conversion are shrouded in some mystery. Constantine is personally responsible for building the foundations of the church in Europe. Before the reign of Constantine the Great, Christianity was persecuted and threatened from every side, yet growing. After his momentous rule of thirty-three years, Christ's authority was endorsed by the secular government, and growth accelerated. Constantine strategically divided his empire and then consolidated power in two critical locations as the church's influence spread across Asia, Europe, and Africa. He also fought against heresy in many forms. His life, while filled with tragedy and triumph, provides some key ideas in the framework of godly leadership and good government. This section will examine Christian persecution in Rome, the life, conversion, and reign of Constantine, his lasting impact on the church, and the relationship between the church and the Just War Theory.

In his book, *The Rise of Christianity*, author and social scientist Rodney Stark (b. 1934) makes the case that among other factors, the church's care for the urban poor and infirmed, respect for women, rapid population increases, and civil disobedience resulted in its growth.[277] He believes that rather than causing or even exacerbating the rise of Christianity, Constantine's reign was the result of the massive increase in the Christian population throughout the Roman Empire in the third century. He acknowledges the role that doctrine and belief had in the attractiveness and strength of this religious movement. Stark discusses the personal benefits, such as purpose, joy, and longevity, that Christians gain. He also downplays the leadership of Constantine in this Christian belief system. This is a constant debate in leadership literature, what are the effects of situation and leader in the outcomes. The Constantine Doctrine proposes that each leader is as a crucial player and their decisions as impactful. Constantine remains a pivotal figure who played an important role in the transformation of the Roman Empire from oppressing Christians to celebrating Christ.

Persecuted

A subtextual theme in this series is the way the church should deal with persecution, especially as a contrast to the use of authoritarian power by Christians. Jesus set expectations for the church when he said, "And you will be hated by all for My name's sake. But he who endures to the end will be saved. When they persecute you in this city, flee to another. For assuredly, I say to you, you will not have gone through the cities of Israel before the Son of Man comes. A disciple is not above his teacher, nor a servant above his master" (Matthew 10:22-24). Each of the Apostles suffered for their faith, and Paul (an Apostle untimely born) may have endured the most. Eloquent as ever, he expressed

---

[277] Stark, R. (2020). The Rise of Christianity: A Sociologist Reconsiders History. United States: Princeton University Press.

his willingness and even eagerness to die as a martyr, "For to me to live is Christ, and to die is gain. If I am to live in the flesh, that means fruitful labor for me. Yet which I shall choose I cannot tell. I am hard-pressed between the two. My desire is to depart and be with Christ, for that is far better. But to remain in the flesh is more necessary on your account" (Philippians 1:21-24). Paul also wrote a message of encouragement to his student and friend Timothy as he contemplated his emanate death, "As for me, I am already being poured out as a drink offering, and the time of my departure has come. I have fought the good fight, I have finished the race, I have kept the faith" (2 Timothy 4:6-7). Devoted and faithful people throughout history have died for the faith.[278]

Paul, during his mission, wanted to visit the church in Rome. "Asking that by God's will I may somehow at last succeed in coming to you. For I am longing to see you so that I may share with you some spiritual gift to strengthen you or rather so that we may be mutually encouraged by each other's faith, both yours and mine. I want you to know, brothers and sisters, that I have often intended to come to you (but thus far have been prevented), in order that I may reap some harvest among you as I have among the rest of the Gentiles" (Romans 1:10-13). Luke wrote of the culmination of Paul's mission in Rome. "He lived there for two whole years at his own expense and welcomed all who came to him, proclaiming the kingdom of God and teaching about the Lord Jesus Christ with all boldness and without hindrance" (Acts 28:29-30). This was Rome under the rule of the psychopathic tyrant Nero (37-68).[279] Through the Apostle Paul,

---

[278] Foxe, J. (1881). Foxe's Book of Martyrs. United States: Claxton.
[279] MacArthur, J. (1997). The Power of Integrity: Building a Life Without Compromise. United States: Crossway.

who laid the groundwork in Rome, God began the mission to evangelize Gentiles.[280] Paul's martyrdom influenced the cultural and religious changes that changed the hearts of an empire and spread across the globe.[281]

Emperor Claudius (10-54), who preceded Nero, expelled Jewish Christians out of the city. Suetonius (69-122), a Roman historian wrote, "Since the Jews constantly made disturbances at the instigation of Christus, he expelled them from Rome."[282] This led to an exodus of those followers of The Way from Rome, including Aquila and Priscilla, a Christian married couple who went to Corinth (see: Acts 18:2). However, in a conflicting source, Claudius only prohibited the gathering of Jewish Christians in meetings both public and private. The Roman historian Cassius Dio (155-235) wrote, "As for the Jews, who had again increased so greatly that because of their multitude it would have been hard without raising a tumult to bar them from the city [Rome], he [Claudius] did not drive them out, but ordered them, while continuing their traditional mode of life, not to hold meetings."[283] Regardless, how could the Christian religion grow under these conditions? Only through the power of the Holy Spirit.

Nero, the most notorious Roman Emperor, blamed the burning of Rome on Christians in 64 AD. He used the Great Fire as an excuse to further persecute the church according to Tacitus.[284]

---

[280] Bruce, F. F. (1977). Paul: apostle of the Free Spirit;" Where the spirit of the Lord is, there the heart is free";(2 Corinthians 3: 17, basic english version). The Paternoster Press.

[281] Allen, R. (1962). Missionary methods: St. Paul's or ours?. Wm. B. Eerdmans Publishing.

[282] Suetonius. The Lives of the Twelve Caesars: Claudius.

[283] Cassius Dio Roman History 60.6.6-7

[284] Dando-Collins, Stephen (2010). The Great Fire of Rome. Da Capo Press. ISBN 978-0-306-81890-5.

While this is disputed by Shaw, the persecution of Christians was an established Roman tradition.[285] "Therefore, to scotch the rumor, Nero substituted as culprits and punished with the utmost refinements of cruelty, a class of men, loathed for their vices, whom the crowd styled Christians. Christus, the founder of the name, had undergone the death penalty in the reign of Tiberius, by sentence of the procurator Pontius Pilatus."[286] We may cobble together some ideas of how Paul died from these fragments. "Owing to envy, Paul also obtained the reward of patient endurance, after being seven times thrown into captivity, compelled to flee, and stoned. After preaching both in the east and west, he gained the illustrious reputation due to his faith, having taught righteousness to the whole world, and come to the extreme limit of the west, and suffered martyrdom under the prefects. Thus, was he removed from the world, and went into the holy place, having proved himself a striking example of patience."[287] While God's calling on Paul's life is unique, not every Christian is the Missionary to the Gentiles, his commitment and self-sacrifice are to be imitated, as he followed Christ's example.

Historical and apocryphal non-canonical books record Paul's execution and the lives of other church fathers. "Then Paul stood with his face to the east and lifted his hands unto heaven and prayed a long time, and in his prayer, he conversed in the Hebrew tongue with the fathers, and then stretched forth his neck without speaking. And when the executioner struck off his head, milk spurted upon the cloak of the soldier. And the soldier and all that were there present when they saw it marveled

---

[285] Shaw, Brent (2015-08-14). "The Myth of the Neronian Persecution". The Journal of Roman Studies. 105: 73–100.
[286] Tacitus Annals 15:44.26-27
[287] I Clement 5.5-7

and glorified God which had given such glory unto Paul: and they went and told Caesar what was done."[288] This is "For the teaching of our Lord [Jesus] at His advent, beginning with Augustus and Tiberius, was completed in the middle of the times of Tiberius. And that of the apostles, embracing the ministry of Paul, ends with Nero."[289] Paul was a Roman citizen trained in Greek philosophy and Jewish law who witnessed to peasants, guards, and kings alike. Peter was crucified on an inverted cross. Stephen was stoned (Acts 7:59). James was murdered at the altar. Historian Tertullian wrote, "We read the lives of the Caesars: At Rome, Nero was the first who stained with blood the rising faith." He continues, "Then does Paul obtain a birth suited to Roman citizenship when in Rome he springs to life again ennobled by martyrdom."[290]

All the apostles were willing to suffer and die for their faith. Thomas died at the orders of the Hindi king Misdeus. He was run through with spears and tossed from a hilltop. The king was mad because Thomas converted his queen Tertia, son Juzanes, sister-in-law princess Mygdonia, and her friend Markia to Christianity. Witnessing to hundreds of people gets you noticed. Sharing your faith with the family of a king can get you killed. Thomas shed his doubts about the power of His Lord and Savior Jesus Christ when he placed his fingers on his savior's nail-pierced hands. Each apostle took the risk to speak of God's truth and love with those in positions of power. As Tertullian wrote in his treatise *Apologeticus* (197 AD), "*Plures efficimur, quitiens metimur a vobis: semen est sanguis Christianorum*" which is often transliterated, "the blood of the martyrs is the seed of the

---

[288] Acts of Paul 11.5
[289] Clement of Alexandria. Stromata. 7.17 (106.3)
[290] Tertullian. Scorpiace 203

church."[291] We must decide how we will resist the Spirit of the Age (see: 2 Corinthians 4:4).

Rod Dreher in his book *Live Not By Lies* details the lives of Christian dissidents from Russia who see the rise of a Chinese-style Social Credit System banning Christians from public life.[292] These systems run by oligarchs, elitists, and government systems are the modern forms of persecution inflicting mental and emotional torture if not physical jail and isolation. For Christian parents, the execution of their children is preferable to their apostasy. All of which leads to forms of enslavement and death by starvation and desperation. Around 2015, multinational corporations shifted their support from the broad middle market to woke capitalism in a move that threatens essential first amendment protections in America. Dreher fears that soft totalitarianism will attack our comfort but may lead us to suffer well and with greater patience. However, many would prefer to retain our freedom and our faith.

Christians may win the spiritual battle either by sacrificing themselves to the hatred of their enemies or standing up for the freedom to fight, suffer, and die if necessary, proving themselves faithful. No one is persecuted for giving in and going along with the demands of an unjust assault. Persecution comes upon those who refuse to bow the knee to idols and lies. At the hands of our persecutors, we will win souls for the kingdom of God. Or, with the power of a sword justly used, protect our lives and land. By promoting love and justice through the channels of government

---

[291] Tertullian, and Robert D. Sider. "Apology." Christian and Pagan in the Roman Empire: The Witness of Tertullian. Washington, D.C.: Catholic University of America, 2001. 8-70.
[292] Dreher, R. (2020). Live Not by Lies: A Manual for Christian Dissidents. United States: Penguin Publishing Group.

we will work toward God's redemptive plan by mitigating evil and encouraging righteousness. Christianity has had a tenuous relationship with power. As Lord John Dalberg-Acton (1834-1902) said, "Power corrupts, and absolute power corrupts absolutely." But managing this tension is part of the calling for Christian leaders.

The fact that Jesus, Paul, and Peter were killed under Roman orders and that same Empire then became the means to spread the gospel to the ends of the earth demonstrates the upside-down nature of God's redemptive plan. The same people motivated by hatred to strike down innocent men laid the foundation for future generations to worship and praise the God they denied. Christians are not supposed to create heaven on earth. We are a preserving, redemptive influence in the world so that more people will come to know Jesus until his return. We can and should use the resources of this planet to increase righteousness, preserve justice, share loving-kindness, and bring peace even as evil plots are hatched against us. But instead of suffering as a martyr, Constantine died in his bed leaving a legacy of forgiveness and faithfulness. God used one man's military skill and political savvy to preserve, protect, and promote the church. Europe transitioned from a battlefield of many rival religions to the seat of a world-altering movement. This happened because of the life of Constantine the Great.

Man, Myth, and Legend

Christian historian Eusebius (~265-340 AD) wrote the definitive contemporaneous biography of Constantine.[293] Many scholars regarded it as biased and possibly propagandistic.

---

[293] Eusebius, (338). Vita Constantini.

While certain facts are incorrect, it remains a reliable source for his life.[294] The practice of celebratory biography or hagiography is an ideological construction of the 19th century because this style was the norm in ancient times.[295] By way of comparison, this factor reinforces the historical reliability of the Gospels which display a balanced view of persons and even the humanity of Jesus Christ (see: Matthew 26:36–56). Empires typically commissioned works that enhanced their power rather than detract from it. While Eusebius' biography is mostly based on his observations with an interview of Constantine later in his life and is oriented toward embellishment, it need not be rejected as completely unreliable in comparison to other ancient sources.

Timothy Baynes, Professor of Classics at the University of Toronto, examined Eusibeus' writing and compared this biography with his assessment of the attitudes in the Roman Empire before Constantine's Christianization of the state. He found that "Constantine... was neither a saint nor a tyrant. He was more humane than some of his immediate predecessors but still capable of ruthlessness and prone to irrational anger."[296] He sought to instill Christian values and principles and to persuade people to worship Christ. "Constantine's character is not wholly enigmatic; with all his faults and despite an intense ambition for personal power, he nevertheless believed sincerely that God had given him a special mission to convert the Roman Empire to Christianity."

---

[294] Hall, S., Cameron, A. (1999). Eusebius' Life of Constantine. United Kingdom: Clarendon Press.

[295] Lifshitz, F. (1994). Beyond Positivism and Genre:"Hagiographical" Texts as Historical Narrative. Viator, 25, 95-114.

[296] Barnes, T. D. (1982). The new empire of Diocletian and Constantine (p. 62). Cambridge, MA: Harvard University Press. Inscriptiones Latinae Selectae 2776.

Constantine's genuine conversion is more probably the case than some contrived story.[297] If he used a false faith for political ends there would be clear indications of limits he placed on the church. Christianity at the time was not strong and popular, so taking on this mantle of weakness belies his strategic skill. Some argue that there were Christians in the army who influenced him. This is unlikely, even if some soldiers were Christian. During the Diocletian persecution (303) the tetrarchy called for the removal of Christians in the nobility and army.[298] Any Christians found in these positions were martyred. Few would have remained by the time Constantine rose to power. His father was not Christian. Even as Christianity expanded in the working classes, it was a distinct minority. Only 15 percent of the Roman population was Christian by the reign of Constantine.[299] Therefore, there was no political advantage to taking on this nascent religion which was generally viewed as a treasonous cult and set against the Roman Empire.

Historians have thus debated whether or not Constantine was Christian or if he truly fought under the banner of the X-P (Chi-Rho) Christogram. Archeological evidence has proven that the Chi-Rho was prominently displayed on coins and tokens from this era, often with the image on a banner flag. This supports the notion that the symbol was important to the Roman Emperor and suggests that he was familiar with the tenets of the faith, and some events motivated his conversion. Constantine was used by God to advance Christianity; he did not use Christianity for

---

[297] Elliott, T. G. (1987). Constantine's Conversion: Do We Really Need It? Phoenix, 41(4), 420–438.

[298] Williams, S. (1996). Diocletian and the Roman recovery. Routledge.

[299] Stephenson, P. (2010). Constantine: Roman Emperor, Christian Victor. Abrams.

his purposes. The Edict of Milan (313), co-authored by Licinius (265-325) a rival Roman general, made Christianity a licit or legal religion.[300] But it did not force Roman citizens to convert. While Licinius' wife was Christian, he likely made sacrifices to Roman gods, inviting prophets and diviners to maintain pagan worship in his court.[301] Constantine negotiated laws with Licinius, but their differences broke down the power-sharing agreement. Eventually, Constantine went to war against Licinius, with his son Crispus commanding the navy.

---

[300] Lenski, N. E. (2012). The Cambridge Companion to the Age of Constantine. United Kingdom: Cambridge University Press.
[301] Ibid.

12

Power Over Life And Death

IT IS DIFFICULT to understand how one would kill another person, let alone order the death of a family member. Constantine and King Solomon both killed family members. The former executed his son and the latter had his brother killed (see: 1 Kings 2:25). Judicial power over life and death is meant to be wielded justly and with humility. Sinful men make hard choices, but Jesus' blood is the only thing that saves lost people, not their righteousness. And the Holy Spirit promotes wisdom and prevents evil actions. Constantine sought a more peaceful society by putting an end to persecution and torture therefore he outlawed crucifixion and gladiators.[302] He also had to deal with the tragic reality of threats to his position. Licinius had attempted to assassinate him, therefore Constantine was on high alert.[303] Fausta, his wife, accused Crispus, his son, of raping her although there are conflicting accounts.[304] These claims sent shock waves through the court.

Emperor Constantine sat as judge in the question of his family member's guilt. Fausta and Crispus were central to his life. Crispus was Constantine's first son by his first wife Minervina.

---

[302] Evers, A. W. H. (2010). Church, Cities, and People: A Study of the Plebs in the Church and Cities of Roman Africa in Late Antiquity. Belgium: Isd.

[303] Barnes, T. D. (1973). Lactantius and Constantine. The Journal of Roman Studies, 63, 29–46.

[304] Hilton, J. L. (2019). Cnemon, Crispus, and the Marriage Laws of Constantine in the Aethiopica of Heliodorus. Greek, Roman, and Byzantine Studies, 59(3), 437-459.

Fausta was his second wife by political necessity as the sister of Emperor Maxentius, one of Constantine's rivals, and was only slightly older than Crispus. It was implied that they had a sexual affair either by consent or rape. It is possible that Fausta unjustly accused Crispus of rape to have him executed and thus allow her son to elevate to the throne.[305] Constantine executed Crispus in 310 on his wife's word and later had Fausta killed in 312 because he doubted her testimony. He may have suffered with what he felt was a rash decision to kill Crispus and felt used by Fausta. According to church historian Philostorgius: "But Constantine, having obtained rule over the whole Roman Empire by remarkable success in wars, ordered his son Crispus to be put to death, at the behest (so people think) of his wife Fausta. Later he locked his wife Fausta in overheated baths and killed her because his mother Helena blamed him out of excessive grief for her grandson."

Zosimus, a Greek historian, wrote, "He killed Crispus, who had been deemed worthy of the rank of Caesar, as I have said before, when he incurred suspicion of having sexual relations with his stepmother Fausta, without taking any notice of the laws of nature. Constantine's mother Helena was distressed at such a grievous event and refused to tolerate the murder of the young man. As if to soothe her Constantine tried to remedy the evil with a greater evil: having ordered baths to be heated above the normal level, he deposited Fausta in them and brought her out when she was dead." Some believe this story is an invention of early Christian writers using adultery to make

---

[305] Wilson, A. E. (1914). The fall of Paganism: a study of the disestablishment of paganism in the establishment of Christianity as the state religion of the Roman Empire (Doctoral dissertation, University of Birmingham).

Constantine's actions acceptable.[306] Constantine killed Fausta's father and brother as his rivals, and she was married to him for over a decade. Fausta bore him six children and he gave her the title Augusta, a very unusual and rare honor. It seems that she betrayed him and then he executed her for it. Sound judgment is required of leaders, and Constantine appears to have made a series of poor choices. He may have been consumed by guilt and regret. Yet, he never remarried after Fausta until he died in 337.

Religious Pluralism

Many religions were allowed in the pagan panoply of religions during the years of Constantine's reign as he consolidated power and supported Christianity.[307] This is the basis of pluralism in Western Civilization, permitting various faiths while promoting the highest truths. Some object to Constantine's faith because of his actions which they claim are contrary to Biblical morality. Some historians have pointed to Constantine's use of capital punishment for his wife and son in the event of treachery, treason, and assassination attempts as an indication of his unregenerate heart. Is Constantine a false Christian because he is not the paragon of virtue? Modern critics of Constantine and other historical figures have a twisted notion that only by meeting the standard of purity can one claim to be a Christian. His life struggles mirror that of a biblical hero. Yet the results of his life show that this warrior general was used by God despite his harsh and demanding position.

---

[306] Woods, D. (1998). On the death of the Empress Fausta. Greece & Rome, 45(1), 70-86.
[307] Cameron, A. (2015). The Mediterranean world in late Antiquity: AD 395-700. Routledge.

Paul was a murderer before his conversion. David was a soldier, adulterer, and murderer during his reign as king. Moses killed a man in defense of his countryman. Joshua was a spy, warrior, and general. Each of these men acted with varying degrees of criminality and these events add perspective to their character. In many ways, Paul's hatred and murder of Christians were the most egregious, and yet his life after his conversion is the most compelling. Many biblical and historical figures had to deal with dirty reality, and faltered along the way. Life and death decisions in the position of judge and king require hard choices. We overplay the case for Christian leaders when we imply that they are sinless. We should understand Christianity as motivating us to sin less. As we are convicted of our sin, we become more aware of areas of our hearts where Christ is not fully king.[308] And in reverence for our God, leaders take more seriously the obligation to make sound decisions even when the alternatives are difficult or ugly.

By seeking to strengthen Christianity, Constantine focused on the same benefits that Stark emphasized. Constantine expanded the social and civil role of women in the church for the benefit of the Roman people.[309] He did not force all Roman citizens to convert to Christianity. Instead, he appealed to the truths of the Christian faith and the efficacy of its tenets. Through his personal experience, witness, and testimony, Constantine made expressions of faith more acceptable and altered the cultural milieu of fourth-century Europe. Christianity was not combined with the Roman Empire under Constantine nor did he make it the official religion of Rome. He supported the faith as an

---

[308] Bridges, J. (2007). Respectable Sins. United States: NavPress.
[309] Stark, R. (1995). Reconstructing the rise of Christianity: The role of women. Sociology of Religion, 56(3), 229-244.

independent entity. In Eusebius' expression of Constantine's leadership, "here for the first time is clearly stated the political philosophy of the Christian Empire."[310] Acting as a morale check against the immoral impulses of secular rulers, the church was to guide leaders into more righteous decision-making.

Constantine's Christian worldview slowly took over the institutions and establishment in Rome. Even with the ambiguity and contradictions inherent in certain decisions to integrate and overturn a pagan society such as building churches in the style of temples, his influence was profound. In 326, Constantine replaced the temple to Venus with a church.[311] Before his conversion, Roman pagan imagery of *Sol Invictus* was on coinage but was later denounced.[312] Pagans, Jews, and Christians all justified the king and his authority by appealing to religious hierarchy. The idea of a singular God is aligned with Judaism, Christianity, and Islam, but not with paganism per se.[313] Therefore, Constantine took monotheism to its logical conclusion using the aqueducts and road systems of the Roman empire to build out the Christian Kingdom through evangelism even at the expense of the emperor's power. Constantine recognized that Rome had already been proven incapable of holding together a crumbling empire. For a secular king in an empire that burned Christians at the stake, fed them to lions, and routinely persecuted them to become a lover of the church and giving up power for the sake of the cross was nothing short of a miracle. The sincerity of his faith is not a function of his

---

[310] Baynes, "Eusebius," 168.

[311] "Church of the Holy Sepulchre, Jerusalem". Jerusalem: Sacred-destinations. com. 21 February 2010. Retrieved 7 July 2012.

[312] Augustine, Sermones, XII; 3:170, n.4 and in Ennaratio in Psalmum XXV; Ennaratio II, 3.

[313] Peterson, 1930 ibid.

righteous acts, it is more likely genuine when we consider the disadvantage of becoming Christian, the early influences in his life, the unusual success he attributed to God, and his efforts to care for the church during his reign.

The Christian Emperor

Born Flavius Valerius Constantinus in the village of Naissus, in what became Nish, Serbia, Constantine was allowed to follow his father's rise to power. He was born on February 27. But the exact year of his birth is unknown, either 271, 272, or 273 AD.[314] His father, Constantius (250-306), was a soldier in the Roman army who excelled to become an officer and eventually became a Caesar in the four-member Tetrarchy.[315] Little is known about his mother, but some speculative accounts paint a humble picture of her influence on the future emperor. Constantine's mother Helena was most likely Greek, may have been born in Bithynia, Asia Minor now modern-day Turkey, and was probably impregnated without formal marriage or if married, under common law.[316] She was referred to as Constantinus' wife and concubine by Jerome.[317] She was a stable maid[318] who raised her child on her own until he was old enough to be educated under Roman schooling.[319]

---

[314] Harbus, Antonia. Helena of Britain in Medieval Legend. Rochester, NY: D.S. Brewer, 2002.
[315] Procopius, Wars of Justinian I.
[316] Barnes, T. D. (1982). The new empire of Diocletian and Constantine (p. 62). Cambridge, MA: Harvard University Press. Inscriptiones Latinae Selectae 2776, cited. p 36.
[317] Jerome. Hieronymus, Chronica, s.a. 292, p. 226, 4 and s.a. 306, p. 228, 23/4, cited in Lieu and Montserrat, 49.
[318] Ambrose, De obitu Theodosii 42; Harbus, 13.
[319] Anonymus Valesianus 1.2, "Origo Constantini Imperatoris"

God may have used a single mother to shape the early life of this powerful leader.[320] She was divorced so that Constantius, Constantine's father, could pursue a more politically advantageous marriage to Theodora the daughter of Augustus Emperor Maximian (250-310). Constantius served under Diocletian (244-311) emperor from 284-305, who established a Tetrarchy where he shared power as Augustus with Maximian and then promoted Galerius (258-311) to Caesar in the east and Constantius Caesar in the west as junior co-emperors. This was a strategic way to manage rivalry and avoid the slaughter and chaos that ensued in military coups and assassinations. Diocletian deftly attempted to use geographic dispersal and military conquest as a distraction for himself and the Tetrarch generals while inter-marriages and child hostages fostered familial bonds. Constantius was occupied with wars against the Franks in Gaul, eventually crossing the English Channel to put down Frankish mercenaries, and then turning his attention to routing the Alemanni, a Germanic tribe along the northern Rhine River. Constantine became the ward of Galerius, his father's equal in rank and contender for the throne.

Constantine was educated, trained, performed his duties, and served well. His position was meant to ensure his father's good conduct while waging war on behalf of Rome. Constantine was raised in Nicomedia, a significant city in the Eastern Roman Empire, in Asia Minor near Byzantium, located in present-day Turkey near Istanbul. His training in Nicomedia included a mixture of Greek, Roman, and Christian teachers, tutors, and reading. Lactantius, a Christian scholar, taught in the academy and streets and may have lectured to the gathered children of nobility. Constantine received a formal education at Diocletian's

---

[320] Drijvers, Helena Augusta, 17–19.

court, where he learned Latin literature, Greek, and philosophy. He eventually joined the Roman legion to follow in his father's footsteps. Constantine served Diocletian and Galerius along the eastern edges of the Roman Empire through Asia. He fought under Diocletian against the Persians in Syria, served tribunates, and fought in Gaul on the Danube River. Under Galerius, Constantine attacked Mesopotamia becoming recognized at a tribune of the first order, a *tribunus ordinis primi*, for his bravery in battle. During this time his father led the campaign in Britain against the Picts.[321]

Diocletian and Galerius sought advice from the oracle of Apollo at Didyma about the continued threat posed by Christians to their power and lifestyle. The palace courtiers overwhelmingly recommended a renewed vigor in the persecution of the church. In Nicomedia, Christians were hunted, captured, and killed under Diocletian while Constantine fought in Europe. Constantine returned home in 303, during the pagan festival of the Terminalia, when the emperor had the church razed, burnt scriptures, and confiscated jewels.[322] This must have left a lasting impression on the young man. Christians were stripped of any rank and title and priests were jailed while Constantine watched, unable to help. He told his biographer that he opposed this horror but could do nothing to prevent it. As panic overtook the city, fires were spread repeatedly torching the royal palace. Galerius blamed this attack on Christians, absent conclusive evidence by a formal investigation, and launched further reprisals.[323] After

---

[321] Carver, M. (2008). Portmahomack: Monastery of the Picts. United Kingdom: Edinburgh University Press.

[322] Barnes, Timothy D. (1981). Constantine & Eusebius. p. 22.

[323] Patricia Southern (2001). The Roman Empire: From Severus to Constantine. p. 168.

executing two eunuchs and six residents who were accused of conspiracy and religious subversion, Galerius declared the palace unfit and dangerous and escaped to Rome.

By 304, Galerius was maneuvering Diocletian and Maximian to promote his nominees, Severus and Maximinus Daia, as Caesars. Constantius asked Galerius to allow Constantine to join him in the west, however, Galerius was cautious and did not release him. According to varied sources, Galerius attempted to have Constantine killed by inserting him into the frontlines of battle, fighting in swamps, and endangering him during hunts or competition.[324] However, he survived every encounter. Constantius' court was built in Gaul, and he again requested that Galerius send his son to join his campaign in Britannia. After an evening party, an intoxicated Galerius granted this call and Constantine left to meet his father that night. He decided to escape immediately to avoid Galerius rescinding his permission, so he rode from messenger post to post, hamstringing every horse in his wake. He met his father in Bononia Gaul and together they traveled across the English Channel to York where the Roman army was assembled at the capital outpost Secunda.[325]

Constantine and his father fought against the polytheistic, pagan, and druidic Celtic Picts beyond Hadrian's Wall for one year. In 305, Diocletian and Maximian announced their retirement at the urging of Galerius allowing him to become Augustus, the top rank, and appoint successors. After a successful campaign, Constantius fell ill and died in York transferring his power to

---

[324] Origo 4; Lactantius, De Mortibus Persecutorum 24.3–9; Praxagoras fr. 1.2; Aurelius Victor 40.2–3; Epitome de Caesaribus 41.2; Zosimus 2.8.3; Eusebius, Vita Constantini 1.21; Lenski, "Reign of Constantine" (CC), 61; MacMullen, Constantine, 32; Odahl, 73.

[325] Bishop, L. (2011). The transformation of administrative towns in Roman Britain (Doctoral dissertation).

his son, making him an Augustus and emperor in the minds of his army. Constantine received acclaim and support from his forces and sent notice to Galerius who was furious but unable to remove him. Instead, he affirmed Constantine but made him Caesar serving under Severus whom he made Augustus of the western half of the empire and co-ruler. Constantine moved to Trier, in southwestern Germany, where he made his home. His ascension meant that he now controlled Britain, Gaul, and Hispania. In 307, in a similar fashion to his father, he married Fausta, Maximian's daughter, for political purposes while separating from his mistress Minervina, who was the mother of his first son, Crispus.

Galerius continued to persecute Christians as Diocletian and Maximian did but failed to eradicate the faith. Instead, he suffered from a horrible gastro-abdominal disease and resorted to begging for aid from the God he hated. Of the Christians, he asked, "Wherefore, for this our indulgence, they ought to pray to their God for our safety, for that of the republic, and their own, that the republic may continue uninjured on every side, and that they may be able to live securely in their homes."[326] Galerius died six days later in 311. Maxentius, the son of Maximian, had grabbed power in Rome in 306 against the wishes of Galerius and secured his position by paying his father's soldiers to abandon the army of Severus. This precipitated a conflict between Constantine and Maxentius in 312.

Constantine converted to Christianity sometime between his father's death and his victory against Maxentius at the Milvian Bridge in 312. His conversion is linked to stories of dreams and

---

[326] Lactantius, "34, 35", De Mortibus Persecutorum [On the Deaths of the Persecutors]

visions. One version has it that upon seeing a cross in the sky while marching through Western Europe in his approach to Rome his army claimed the mantle of Christ.[327] Some scholars have attributed this symbol to an astrological event such as the alignment of Mars, Saturn, Jupiter, and Venus in the constellations Capricorn and Sagittarius.[328] This account strains credulity and reeks of similar reasoning applied to the Star of Bethlehem in the Christmas story as a comet[329] or planetary conjunction.[330] It is a stretch to ascertain that this symbol was a solar halo.[331] Other naturalistic explanations of miracles have been offered for the parting of the Red Sea during the Hebrew Exodus.[332] For any miraculous event there are essentially three options: 1) It happened because of God as told 2) It just happened to occur naturally at the time it was needed or 3) It did not happen and thus was an entirely made up and manufactured support for the agenda of the people involved. Certainly, the latter has happened throughout history, but these invented stories do not carry the same weight as Biblical signs and often fade into myth or are forgotten. Option two seeks apparent compatibility between natural events and miraculous signs. Both options one and two require God to orchestrate events to accomplish his

---

[327] Eusebius, Vita Constantini III.

[328] Michael DiMaio, Jörn Zeuge, and Natalia Zotov, "Ambiguitas Constantiniana: The Caeleste Signum Dei of Constantine the Great," Byzantion 58 (1988) 333-60.

[329] "Star of Bethlehem." Cross, F. L., ed. The Oxford dictionary of the Christian Church. New York: Oxford University Press. 2005.

[330] Telegraph (2008-12-09), "Jesus was born in June", The Daily Telegraph, London, retrieved 2011-12-14.

[331] Peter Weiss, The vision of Constantine, Journal of Roman Archeology 16 (2003), 237–259.

[332] Drews, Carl; Han, Weiqing (3 April 2007). "No, really: There is a scientific explanation for the parting of the Red Sea in Exodus". The Washington Post. Retrieved 21 May 2017.

purpose or some amazing coincidence. Option three reads facts back into history and does not make sense of data concerning Constantine's spiritual transformation after this event.

The Emblem of Christ Appearing to Constantine, by Rubens (1622)

Historians generally shrink from supernatural explanations for events, it is uncomfortable to attribute God's hand in Constantine's success. Biographer Ian Hughes (b. 1951) makes the case that Constantine's military prowess and generalship deserve equal if not greater praise than his religious reforms.[333] Visions are not equivalent to God sending fire from heaven. A dream indicates that changing this general's heart

---

[333] Hughes, I. (2021). A Military Life of Constantine the Great. United Kingdom: Pen and Sword.

was the target of God. Lactantius, a Roman Christian tutor to Constantine's son, Crispus, wrote that before the Battle of the Milvian Bridge Constantine received instructions in his dream to place the sign of Christ, the Chi-Rho, on his army's banners and shields. Eusebius recalls the story of this dream and the Chi-Rho symbol. He added that during the march toward Rome prior to this dream a cross of light appeared in the sky before his army with the words in *hoc signo vinces* (In this sign, you will conquer.).[334] The battle standard of the Chi-Rho was used and became known as the labarum. It is undisputed that on October 28, 312 Constantine approached the Milvian Bridge, a crucial logistical point in the defense of Rome. He anticipated that Maxentius would bunker the city and endure a siege but instead, the emperor met him at the entrance to the bridge which was already partially destroyed and buoyed by floating pieces. Constantine's well-trained cavalry routed Maxentius' cavalry and with no path for ordered retreat, his army pushed the infantry and Praetorian guard into the Tiber River where Maxentius was drowned. Constantine gave "the God of the Christians" all glory for his victory and praised him before his army.

---

[334] Haaren, John H.; Poland, A. B. (2006) [1904]. Famous Men of Rome. Yesterday's Classics. p. 229. ISBN 978-159915-046-8.

13

The Risen Christ

CONSTANTINE'S VICTORY AT the Milvian Bridge solidified his reign and laid the foundation of Christian Europe in the west and including the spread of Christianity through the eastern portion of the continent. This led to centuries of church influence in politics and culture. Literature and laws were shaped by Christian theological and doctrinal issues and debates. From Greece to Russia the church became a stabilizing force, establishing bulkheads on the eastern front of Europe. The continent was preserved through the Middle Ages, was reborn in the Renaissance, and flourished in the Age of Exploration under great stress and strain, as detailed in *The Columbus Initiative*. Christian ethics mitigated the worst instincts of liberalization. Science and technology expanded the reach of Western Civilization to America where these same conflicts were recapitulated under the rubric of a biblical worldview for hundreds of years, as detailed in *The Lincoln Legacy*. We should learn from Constantine's actions and make an example of his leadership. The first war waged by a Christian on behalf of the church were the battles to consolidate the Roman Empire under Constantine.

No leader between the ascension of Christ and the formation of the early church of Acts had sought or acquired national power. Peter, James, and John each had a leadership role to play in the church, but their holy ambition ended with their ministry and martyrdom. Saul, who became Paul, the apostle who wrote the largest portion of the New Testament and developed key doctrines, spent more time in a jail cell than in a throne room. But somehow the religion that was credited by Augustine and Tertullian for bringing down the Roman Empire became the primary faith held by peasants, military, and nobility during its crumbling demise. The Republic's motto SPQR, *Senātus Populusque Rōmānus*, "The Senate and People of Rome" was the emblem for the government which was supposed to abide by its citizens. Less than 150 years after the reign of Constantine, the empire fell but reforming its principles continued. In the ashes of a nation judged for its failures and abuses rose a faith that expanded across the continent and testified throughout the world. The history of Christianity as a religion is the history of the Church as a body of believers which has taken many shapes and forms. Protestants, Catholics, and Orthodox Christians all share a common past in the formation and rise of the church in Europe.

In one of the most incisive analyses of Eusebius' writings, Devin Singh (b. 1977) makes a clear case for the orthodoxy of Eusebius theology and the motivations of his political positions.[335] In *The Life of Constantine* connections drawn between God and the emperor are mediated by the Logos, which is another name for the incorporeal second person of the trinity, Jesus Christ. The endorsement of Constantine as a leader in a church is justified by his submission to the lordship of Christ while seeking redemption, forgiveness, and sanctification. Singh goes on to speculate that in many letters to royal children: "The ideal portrait of the emperor serves less as flattery than as a standard to which his sons are called and displays understandable

---

[335] Singh, D. (2015). Eusebius as political theologian: The legend continues. Harvard Theological Review, 108(1), 129-154.

distance from reality." Further in *The Laudation of Constantine*, Eusebius deftly uses his rhetorical skill to craft a hyperbolic faithfulness attributed to Constantine while holding him accountable to the values and virtues he professed. A plausible argument is made that Eusebius was not simply lying when he withheld facts, but instead, he buttressed the future church and helped shape its governance by painting the most positive picture of a man who, while flawed, performed great deeds like many people in Christian history.

Yet, scholars continue to criticize the authenticity of Constantine's faith. Some reference the fact that he was essentially baptized on his deathbed. But it is not concerning that Constantine delayed his baptism until he neared his death, many Christians during the early church age erroneously treated baptism like their last rites.[336] He may have been moved toward Christianity well before 312.[337] By 326, Constantine became the sole emperor of a unified Rome. But Christianity did not become the official state religion of the Empire until 380 well after his death in 337. Celebrating his influence is not an endorsement of a unified church and state, but clarion calls for Christian leadership in a secular government to protect the best aspects of our society and culture. Some scholars have claimed that he forced people to accept Christ and the church as the only faith.[338] However, when he issued the Edict of Milan it made Christianity a legal religion along with all other licit forms of belief. He decriminalized faith and offered a pluralist

---

[336] A. H. M. Jones, The Later Roman Empire (Oxford 1964) 981

[337] Barnes, T. D. (1985). The conversion of Constantine. Echos du monde classique: Classical views, 29(3), 371-391.

[338] Drake, H. A. (2006). The impact of Constantine on Christianity. The Cambridge companion to the age of Constantine, 113.

view of religion that invited many sects into the public square. Constantine did promote Christianity throughout his reign, spreading a moderately new religion to the edges of the Roman Empire and removing pagan rituals, but did not persecute unbelievers.[339]

In his endorsement of Christianity, he set into motion a philosophical revolution between government leaders and their creator. God was the ultimate being, fully other, and should be worshiped. But Roman citizens, like many cultures before them and around the world, considered their ruler a divine being. Constantine and the followers of Christ considered Jesus to be the only son of God, King of kings, and Lord of lords. Man would serve God in leadership roles but must never claim to be divine. This distinction would take centuries to work its way into the hearts and minds of Europeans, giving rise to the American democratic movement, and eventually making progress around the world. While freedom rose in fits and starts, the transformation of government continues to this day and faces many dire challenges. Be that as it may, the Christian confidence in one God, who was sovereign over creation but does not rule any one nation, made the head of state accountable to Christ.

Authority in the Roman empire was to be shared by the Senate and Caesar, whenever Caesar took dictatorial power then the Senate would thwart, execute, or remove him. Authority is the right to command obedience and action.[340] Later, in the Roman Catholic Church, authority was vested in the Pope through

---

[339] Billirakis, M. N. (1975). The religious character of Constantine I, the Great (Doctoral dissertation, [Youngstown, Ohio]: Youngstown State University, 1975.).
[340] Blass, T. (1999). The milgram paradigm after 35 years: Some things we now know about obedience to authority 1. Journal of applied social psychology, 29(5), 955-978.

the hierarchy of cardinals and priests. Church ecclesiastical polity refers to the structure of organizational, administrative, and operational relationships in a particular denomination or tradition. Every organization of people includes relationships as a source of influence for leadership. Therein are the bases of power and sources of authority.[341] Power is "simply the ability to get things done the way one wants them to be done."[342] The delegation of power shifts authority and responsibility for action to lower levels of a hierarchical organization when done properly. Constantine demonstrated his influence through a keen use of power while delegating and decentralizing it.

Constantine split the Roman Empire into two halves, east and west, governed from two separate cities Rome and Constantinople. This politically savvy move presaged the fall of the Empire in toto while preserving Christian influence. And this distributed power more broadly rather than maintaining the concentration of wealth and authority in a city infested with Senators and rebels. His move was essentially to disassemble the administrative state and mitigate the damage that special interest groups could wreak on the nation. The western half was seated in Rome and the eastern half was seated in Constantinople which has become modern-day Istanbul. Constantine named the city Nova Roma and began rebuilding walls, ports, and trade routes. His life in Nicomedia and experiences throughout Asia Minor made him very familiar with the strategic importance of this port city and choke point.

---

[341] French, J. R., Raven, B., & Cartwright, D. (1959). The bases of social power. Classics of organization theory, 7, 311-320.
[342] Salancik, G. R., & Pfeffer, J. (1989). Who Gets Power and How They Hold on to it: A Strategic-Contingency Model of Power. Readings in managerial psychology, 346.

Leaders must deal with the question of when and how to centralize power or delegate it to others. While it may seem appealing for followers to have leaders always divest power, this is not in the best interest of the group. Henri Fayol (1841-1925), one of the early and prominent management scientists, in his principles of management[343] described many of the same principles of bureaucracy and hierarchy espoused by sociologist Max Weber (1864-1920).[344] Essentially, both recommend order, a clear chain of command, job specialization, and controls. The Roman Senate exerted greater control in the capital city and set up the tetrarchy system where one emperor was kept close and under control by the Praetorian guard paid by the Senate. Then vice-regent Caesars and Augustus would compete for power while waging war on the edges of the empire, preventing them from gaining influence at home. A state bureaucracy allows individuals to hide behind departments and agencies avoiding responsibility and even engaging in criminal conduct.[345] Modern business management professors such as Richard Daft (b. 1941) emphasize the tension between unified strategic action and the need for information and communication at the lowest levels of any organization.[346] The United States attempted to solve this problem by emphasizing local control of legal and political matters through federalism.

Delegation is highly important. Constantine's plan would be like a US President spreading out the access and proceeds of

---

[343] Fayol, H. (1916). General principles of management. Classics of organization theory, 2(15), 57-69.

[344] Weber, M. (1946). Bureaucracy. From Max Weber: essays in sociology, 196, 232-235.

[345] Merton, R. K. (1963). Bureaucratic structure and personality.

[346] Daft, R. L. (2012). Organization Theory and Design. United States: Cengage Learning.

Washington, D.C., throughout the country based on an assessment of the links between location and industry. This move would especially empower member states and individuals over aspects of the federal budget. Under President Donald Trump, David Bernhardt signed Secretary's Order (SO) 3382 formally establishing the Bureau of Land Management's (BLM) headquarters in Grand Junction, Colorado, where the agency would be closer to the land that it oversees.[347] President Joe Biden undid this action.[348] Why are most agencies entrenched in Washington, DC? Presumably to be closer to power. More likely to provide access to influence peddling and high-paying jobs for friends and family members of well-connected politicians. This effort to decentralize through presidential fiat is weak, but it could be formalized by forcing relocations, incorporating clear lines of communication and authority in all regional offices by federal law.

The United States Federal Bank has twelve districts, but each acts as an arm of the Central Bank. If they were able to more independently manage economic growth based on regional differences the power of the Fed would decrease. If Alabama were to take on all purchasing for the military fewer contractors would set up shop in the D.C. metro area. If the FBI and CIA headquarters were moved to the heartland in Michigan, Indiana, or Ohio our law enforcement would more closely reflect the interests of the nation and not our capital. If the IRS was in West Virginia the mentality of tax authority would change. If Tulsa, Oklahoma; Cincinnati, Ohio; Chico, California; Bangor, Maine;

---

[347] https://www.blm.gov/press-release/The-Bureau-of-Land-Management-Headquarters-Officially-Established-in-Grand-Junction-Colorado
[348] https://www.blm.gov/press-release/secretary-haaland-outlines-next-steps-rebuild-bureau-land-management

and Juno, Alaska all shared aspects of the EPA functions, environmental policy would have greater consideration for local concerns. K-street lobbyists would lose interest in many projects where the implementation dollars and jobs take them to far-flung states. Decentralizing the administration of the national government would have a similar effect to splitting the Roman Empire, it may preserve the purpose of our union.

States would benefit from federal jobs held by local citizens who would more closely share the values of their immediate surroundings. To protect our states from the undue influence of the federal government, employment must be decoupled from federal employee unions and instead rest more with state elected officeholders. Any efforts at decentralization start with the OPM, Office of Personnel Management, and would meet resistance.[349] But change requires the ability to build urgency, set a vision for the future, create a guiding coalition, and press on to a satisfactory conclusion.[350] Changing these agencies would modernize the government and create more equitable economic incentives. This way no job is guaranteed for life nor are pensions guaranteed, but instead, all Americans have similar opportunities, and appointed positions serve at the pleasure of federal and state administrations. Understanding our common history will lead to some key agreements and highlights disagreements that persist to this day.

The Fall of Rome

Constantine was the first Christian to gain secular power. The Kingdom of God was never meant to be an earthly reign

---

[349] Moffit, R. E. (2019) OPM'S Multi-State Plan Program: Time to Say Goodbye. www.Heritage.org

[350] Kotter, J. P. (2012). Leading change. Harvard business press.

of men. Instead, God used imperfect people to accomplish His holy agenda. Constantine is such a man that was used by God to elevate Christianity. He protected many people from threats and harm to reform the secular and polytheistic culture of Rome. Constantine's mother Helena became a Christian while in his court in Rome.[351] As Christianity rose the Roman Empire crumbled. With the Edict of Milan in 313 which permitted the practice of Christianity the center of power in the empire shifted and moral laws were instituted, essentially creating a peace agreement between the spiritual invasion of this religion and the resistance of the faltering earthly kingdom. Constantine provided his mother Helena safe passage to Jerusalem where she presumably located The cross of Jesus Christ and other relics with the help of Eusebius and Macarius.[352] In 327, Constantine and his mother Helena separately commissioned the Church of the Nativity in Bethlehem.[353] When Christianity became the state religion in 380, the empire was well on a path to ruin.[354]

Many claim that the disintegration of Roman values led to this collapse because of an immoral rot from within. Edward Gibbon (1737-94), the preeminent enlightenment scholar of Rome wrote, "The vigor of the military government was relaxed, and finally dissolved, by the partial institutions of Constantine; and the Roman world was overwhelmed by a

---

[351] S. Borgehammar, "How the Cross was found, from event to medieval legend," Bibliotheca Theologiae Practicae 47 (Stockholm 1991) 54-5 and J.W. Drijvers, Helen Augusta: the mother of Constantine the Great and the legend of her finding the True Cross (Leiden 1991).

[352] Owen, G. Frederick, ed. (1983) [1964]. The Thompson Chain-Reference Bible (Fourth improved (updated) ed.). Indianapolis: B.B. Kirkbride Bible Co. p. 323 (appendix).

[353] McMahon, Arthur L. (1913). "Holy Sepulchre". In Herbermann, Charles (ed.). Catholic Encyclopedia. New York: Robert Appleton Company.

[354] https://www.history.com/news/8-reasons-why-rome-fell

deluge of Barbarians."[355] Gibbon's comprehensive work has been addressed by many; his claim that the church caused a loss of civic virtue and weakness that preceded the fall of Rome is a suspect explanation. Christianity replaced a failing national ethos by upending a weak and impotent religious myth with a more sustainable and powerful theology. Other than Christianity, only Islam has created and sustained a transnational empire for over 1000 years. Roman values included respect for a sovereign and divine king. Shifting the focus of people away from their earthly emperor and toward a spiritual God was a radical change. According to Gibbon, when the Pope, bishops, and priests gained political power the administration of a widespread empire ruled by force of arms and taxation was weakened.[356] Christianity contributed to reforming Roman values, military, and economy but its problems were more significant than that.

Rome had already been under consistent attack and remained on a war footing throughout its decline. Polybius' Histories recorded the reaction of General Scipio Aemilianus to the burning of Carthage (146 BC) cried, *"Carthago deleta fuit"* (Carthage has been destroyed). This portended the eventual destruction of Rome as he recognized that "A day will come when sacred Troy shall perish, and Priam and his people shall be slain."[357] It is wrong to call this a prediction of the fall of the

---

[355] Gibbon, Edward (1911). The History of the Decline and Fall of the Roman Empire, Volume 5. London. pp. 391–392. In Chapter 38 "General Observations on the Fall of the Roman Empire in the West."

[356] Gibbon, E. (1843). The history of the decline and fall of the Roman Empire (Vol. 2). Harper & brothers.

[357] Rood, T. (2004). Polybius. In Narrators, Narratees, and Narratives in Ancient Greek Literature (pp. 147-164). Brill.

Western Empire some 600 years later.[358] Instead, it should be clear that even the generals of this great nation were aware of its internal contradictions. Constantine was an accomplished general and skilled politician. Under his command, the Roman military vanquished Licinius, in 324, and unified the empire. But Constantine seemed to anticipate the complete threat that Scipio foresaw. By authorizing a division of the Empire into two sections he attempted to preserve the influence of Christianity by divesting power out of Rome.

Rome depended on slave labor which led to it becoming vulnerable to labor shortages, revolts, and uprisings. When Constantine divided the empire, he did so to avoid the stranglehold that Rome had on national policy. This decentralization also accompanied the segmentation of authority into two seats of royal power which eventually broke apart the unity of the church which was attached to state endorsements. However, the Great Schism was the first major challenge and altered the ecclesiology of the Roman Catholic Church to undercut papal authority. This presaged the Protestant Reformation which focused on biblical authority rather than replacing earthly and human leadership. Attacks on the outskirts of the empire led Emperor Hadrian (76-138) to build a wall to prevent Pict raids on outposts thus extending resources to the edges of supply lines only for raw conquest. Constantine experienced this firsthand. The corruption of the Senate and Praetorian Guard led Constantine to disband this supposedly protective force which had proven capable of executing a coup d'état. The fall culminated when Germanic tribes, many of whom were trained as Roman mercenaries, fought against their masters. Constantine

---

[358] Polybius. Histories, Book 38.

fought the Goths who rejected Roman rule in 300. In 410, Visigoths led by King Alaric, a German warlord, sacked Rome. The empire lingered as Vandals attacked between 455-476 until Romulus Augustulus was defeated by the general Odoacer.

Did not Christianity contribute to the fall of the Roman Empire? The ascent of the Christian religion ran against the prevailing ethos of Rome. As a monotheistic faith, it contradicted the polytheistic religions of Greek and Roman traditions. Paul at Mars Hill challenged these pagan religions directly: "Now while Paul was waiting for them at Athens, his spirit was provoked within him as he saw that the city was full of idols. So, he reasoned in the synagogue with the Jews and the devout persons, and in the marketplace every day with those who happened to be there. Some of the Epicurean and Stoic philosophers also conversed with him. And some said, 'What does this babbler wish to say?' Others said, 'He seems to be a preacher of foreign divinities'— because he was preaching Jesus and the resurrection. And they took him and brought him to the Areopagus, saying, 'May we know what this new teaching is that you are presenting? For you bring some strange things to our ears. We wish to know therefore what these things mean.'

"Now all the Athenians and the foreigners who lived there would spend their time in nothing except telling or hearing something new. So Paul, standing in the Areopagus, said: 'Men of Athens, I perceive that in every way you are very religious. For as I passed along and observed the objects of your worship, I found also an altar with this inscription: "To the unknown god." What therefore you worship as unknown, this I proclaim to you. The God who made the world and everything in it, being Lord of heaven and earth, does not live in temples made by man, nor is he served by human hands, as though he needed anything since he himself gives to all mankind life and breath and everything. And he made from one man every nation of mankind to live yon all the face of the earth, having determined allotted periods and the boundaries of their dwelling place, that they should seek God, and perhaps feel their way toward him and find him. Yet he is actually not far from each one of us, for 'In him we live and move and have our being'; as even some of your own poets have said, 'For we are indeed his offspring.' Being then God's offspring, we ought not to think that the divine being is like gold or silver or stone, an image formed by the art and imagination of man. The times of ignorance God overlooked, but now he commands all people everywhere to repent, because he has fixed ma day on which he will judge the world in righteousness by a man whom he has appointed; and of this He has given assurance to all by raising Him from the dead" (Acts 17:22-31).

However, the way that the Christian religion functioned gives us insight into the differences between a cultic pagan system and a theistic moral worldview. Roman oppression of Christians and slaves reduced rebellions and education that would have led to greater freedom and equality for all people.[359] By endorsing Christianity in 313, Constantine changed this and abdicated his position as a god. Did the Roman people ever really believe that a general or orator became divine simply because they occupied the seat of power? Probably not, demonstrating the damage that an internal contradiction does to religion. If a belief system is driven with vapid and hollow reasoning it will only produce compliance at the cost of cognitive dissonance. This reinforces rather than overturns entrenched beliefs even if

---

[359] Goodman, M. (1993). The ruling class of Judaea: the origins of the Jewish revolt against Rome, AD 66-70. Cambridge University Press.

they are incorrect.[360] One of the tragedies of Western Civilization is that Christianity has had to protect itself from false teachers who strike at the foundation of a worldview that offers the most reliable and comprehensive explanations to our deepest questions. The Christian faith in the One True Creator God, Maker of Heaven and Earth, spelled the end to mandates and dictates from earthly rulers. This God, no longer viewed as a Jewish tribal deity, led Constantine to end the persecution, torture, and murder of thousands of Christians. Instead, Christianity was elevated from cult status to a position of prominence in the Roman world. While Constantine did not make Christianity the official state religion of the Empire he allowed it to grow and flourish as an alternative to the ensconced religious practice.

This triumph of human reasoning and logical thinking over superstition is monumental. Most atheists rightly reject overly superstitious practices of varied religious traditions. Modern debates between Christian traditions about the differences between sacraments and ordinances borders between superstition and the supernatural. Our sinful nature and religious instincts have led mankind to make horrific and foolish appeals to the gods such as child sacrifice and war. But honoring and respecting the supernatural aspects of life is not the same as feeding superstitions. The mystical experiences that all humans seek have found expression in nature, family, and drug-induced stupors. People throughout history used leaves, plants, seeds, and alcohol to alter their state of consciousness.[361] These

---

[360] Festinger, L. (1962). Cognitive dissonance. Scientific American, 207(4), 93-106.
[361] Pollan, M. (2018). How to Change Your Mind: What the New Science of Psychedelics Teaches Us About Consciousness, Dying, Addiction, Depression, and Transcendence. United States: Penguin Publishing Group.

transcendent universal experiences are oddly similar and tap into our need to relate with others and God. Christianity promoted an altered state of being, not only consciousness, without psychedelics, where our lives of prayer and communion with the Holy Spirit transform our motivations and desires. An extraordinary change in religion led faith to become individualized yet unified, matching personal accountability with the community and spreading this burgeoning religion to the edge of the empire.

14

Just War Theory

CHRISTIANITY WAS PRIMARILY expanded through self-sacrifice. Initially, the religion grew with Christians sharing the gospel through interpersonal interactions while being persecuted as martyrs. Secondarily, as Christians built a society of industrious warriors, the church grew through exploration and conquest by individuals and the state. Warfighting and its justification is the last area of Constantine's life that must be examined, and this will inform future discussions on related topics. Is it possible for Christians to conduct earthly warfare by killing enemies of a secular state? In 426, Augustine of Hippo developed the Just War Theory which details the conditions under which Christians can and should engage in war.[362] He pointed out that while Christians often suffered and died rather than taking up arms, following the example of Jesus' crucifixion, self-defense and defending a nation are acceptable, legitimate, and even at times encouraged by the church. This argument has been divided into two categories, the "right to go to war" (*jus ad bellum*) and "right conduct in war" (*jus in bello*).[363] An American Christian soldier must have a just rationale for war, no prohibitions against a particular action, and conduct war according to the uniform code of military justice.

---

[362] Augustine of Hippo. City of God.
[363] Guthrie, Charles; Quinlan, Michael (2007). "III: The Structure of the Tradition". Just War: The Just War Tradition: Ethics in Modern Warfare. pp. 11–15. ISBN 978-0747595571.

Augustine integrated the biblical, Greek, and Roman views on war.[364] Laws of war existed in ancient Israel (see: Deuteronomy 23:10) and Greek states had some unwritten norms that regulated the aspects of warfare such as neutrality, dates, and locations of battle.[365] Plato saw war as inevitable where Aristotle built an ethic of war around the laws of nature which was expanded upon by Cicero.[366] The Romans made warfare into a national pastime. Cicero said, "Now since there are two ways of contesting for a decision, one by discussion, the other by force, and since the former is proper for man, the latter for beasts, one should have recourse to the latter only if it is impossible to use the former. Wars, then, are to be waged in order to render it possible to live in peace without injury."[367] In *De Republica,* he continued, "Those wars are unjust which are undertaken without cause. Now without a purpose to punish wrong or to beat back an attacking enemy, no just war can be waged."[368]

Augustine's development of the Just War Theory dovetailed with Cicero and was echoed by Thomas Aquinas (1225-1274) who wrote extensively on natural law as described by Aristotle.[369] Hugo Grotius (1583–1645) in his book *On the Law of War and Peace* shared this same assessment of warfare combining secular

---

[364] Lenihan, D. A. (1988). The just war theory in the work of Saint Augustine. Augustinian Studies, 19, 37-70.

[365] Lanni, A. (2008). The Laws of War in Ancient Greece. Law and History Review, 26(3), 469-489.

[366] Reichberg, G., Syse, H., & Begby, E. (2006). The ethics of war: classical and contemporary readings.

[367] Harrer, G. A. (1918). Cicero on Peace and War. The Classical Journal, 14(1), 26–38.

[368] Cicero, M. T. (46 BC). On the Commonwealth. United States.

[369] Elders, L. (2019). The Ethics of St. Thomas Aquinas: Happiness, Natural Law, and the Virtues. United States: Catholic University of America Press.

and religious reasoning to restrain violence.[370] Michael Walzer (b. 1935) in his landmark book *Just and Unjust War* details how the use of asymmetrical warfare against terrorists and insurgents requires arguments on proportionality and morality in the conduct of war.[371] But he avoids discussions about the causes of war because often they are obfuscated by personal and national interests.

Religious disputes may lead to family feuds, civic divisions, and even national wars in some cases.[372] Throughout history, conflicts have stemmed from differences in what people believe. Jealousy, revenge, and gluttony promote interpersonal violence, but ideology motivates tyrants to subjugate masses of people with armies of war. Good men and women must fight against these threats for the sake of truth, honor, and justice which find their ultimate expression in God and his law. We live in an era of global conflicts between religions, secular movements, and localized sectarian violence.[373] Many wars, like the Balkan genocide where Muslim families were killed, have a religious component, but ethnic and tribal motives often provide the strategic impetus for territorial expansion.[374] It must be noted that personal, economic, tribal, and geopolitical factors have

---

[370] Grotius, H. (1625). De jure belli ac pacis libri tres: Prolegomena. United Kingdom: Clarendon Press.

[371] Walzer, M. (2015). Just and Unjust Wars: A Moral Argument with Historical Illustrations. United States: Basic Books.

[372] Svensson, I. (2012). Ending Holy Wars: Religion and Conflict Resolution in Civil Wars. Australia: University of Queensland Press.

[373] Ramsay, G. (2016). Dehumanisation in religious and sectarian violence: the case of Islamic State. Global Discourse, 6(4), 561-578.

[374] Cigar, N. L., Meštrović, S. G. (1995). Genocide in Bosnia: The Policy of "ethnic Cleansing". Cambodia: Texas A&M University Press.

contributed more than religion to wars throughout history.[375] Christians became acting soldiers in the Roman military under Christian emperors without an endorsement of the emperor as supreme ruler. After Constantine, Caesar was no longer viewed as divine or divinely appointed.

A Christian General

Constantine aligned himself with Jesus Christ in the battle of the Milvian Bridge using the Chi-Rho labarum as a sign of protection. He won a miraculous victory while outnumbered in the Battle of Cibalae (316) against Licinius.[376] As with all history, this can be attributed either to God's hand or the general's military skill, certainly, a Christian historian's interpretations will consider both human behavior and divine intervention while downplaying chance and fate.[377] Later, his victory at Chrysopolis near Byzantium solidified his efforts to consolidate the empire under his leadership and reorganize its structure.[378] Military victories were recounted with mosaics depicting Christian imagery rather than pagan. Jesus is likely portrayed alongside Constantine and his son in the Archiepiscopal Chapel at Ravenna depicting the passage, "Thou shalt tread upon the lion and adder: the young lion and the dragon shalt thou trample under

---

[375] O'brien, S. P. (2010). Crisis early warning and decision support: Contemporary approaches and thoughts on future research. International studies review, 12(1), 87-104.

[376] Mirković, M. (2012). Co-Regency: Constantine and Licinivs and the political division of the Balkans. Zbornik radova Vizantoloskog instituta, (49), 7-18.

[377] Greek and Roman Historiography in Late Antiquity: Fourth to Sixth Century A.D.. (2003). Netherlands: Brill.

[378] Odahl, C. (2010). Constantine and the Christian Empire. United Kingdom: Taylor & Francis.

feet" (Psalm 91:13).[379] The results of Constantine's reign are seen in the decades and centuries after his death. An important but hotly disputed source, *The Anonymus Valesianus* (1636) details the lineage of Constantine by 474 AD and the fall of Rome in the rise of the Ostrogothic king Theoderic.[380] Theoderic was seduced by Arian heresy and supported the false Pope Symmachus, who ordered the seizure of Catholic basilicas by Arians when he was stricken and killed by a "loose stomach."[381]

Man is inherently religious so there are many different interpretations of spiritual reality. These debates should be resolved peaceably rather than at the point of a sword.[382] From monotheism and deism to polytheism or atheism, our disagreements about the ultimate nature of reality spark conflagrations. Variances in belief point to the underlying nature of man—that all religions ask similar questions and yet come to different answers. As discussed, different views about spiritual reality tend to center on common themes. However, the sinful nature of man has incited rivalry, greed, and hatred between people groups which has been galvanized by ambitious leaders. Anthropology and theology interact; our understanding of humanity impacts religious beliefs and vice versa. Christianity has a reserved view of humanity acknowledging that original sin perverts and pollutes our thoughts and actions. Pelagius (c. 350-c. 425), an ascetic British monk and heretic condemned

---

[379] Bardill, J., Bardill, R. F. (2012). Constantine, Divine Emperor of the Christian Golden Age. United Kingdom: Cambridge University Press.

[380] Elton, H. (2018). The Roman Empire in Late Antiquity: A Political and Military History. United Kingdom: Cambridge University Press.

[381] Adams, J. N. (1976). The text and language of a vulgar latin chronicle (anonymus valesianus ii). Bulletin Supplement (University of London. Institute of Classical Studies), iii-189.

[382] Ibid. Svensson

by the Council of Chalcedon (431 AD), denied this doctrine that "sin came into the world through one man, and death through sin, and so death spread to all men because all sinned (Romans 5:12)." In *A Conflict of Visions*, Thomas Sowell addresses the way that societies' view of human nature, either "constrained" by limits like sin or "unconstrained" naïvely utopian, affects decisions including those on war.[383] These "ideological origins of political struggles" have been accentuated by atheist Steven Pinker (b. 1954) in *The Blank Slate*. He attributes them to evolutionary psychological adaptations that Christians assign to our spiritual and moral nature and limitations.[384]

The Origins of War

Many evolutionary scientists and psychologists have attempted to ground mankind's propensity to fight, and on occasion cooperate, in biological and genetic factors exemplified in primate behavior. However ecological not psychological factors were most salient when instigating territorial aggression in adult male chimpanzees (*Pan troglodytes*).[385] Bret Weinstein (b. 1969), an evolutionary biologist, proposes that "variation in commitment to the group can be explained by a rule of stability-dependent cooperation, where the adaptive level of individual commitment varies inversely with the stability of the social

---

[383] Sowell, Thomas (2007) [First published 1987]. A Conflict of Visions: Ideological Origins of Political Struggles (Revised ed.). Basic Books. ISBN 978-0-465-00205-4.

[384] Pinker, Steven (2002), The Blank Slate: The Modern Denial of Human Nature, New York: Penguin Books.

[385] Gilby IC, Wilson ML, Pusey AE. Ecology rather than psychology explains co-occurrence of predation and border patrols in male chimpanzees. Anim Behav. 2013 Jul;86(1):61-74.

group."[386] Less stable groups have more conflict. And durable social systems like Christianity promote peace. Robert Trivers (b. 1943), sociobiologist and professor at Rutgers University, has postulated that human self-deception is uniquely suited to creating the conditions for war.[387] This is particularly true when tribal distinctions between family and enemies are based on in-group vs out-group preferences.

Often religious divisions are related to tribal group preferences. Vertical dyad linkages, unique relationships between individuals in a group, led to the development of the Leader-Member Exchange Theory (LMX) to explain group decision-making under great stress such as that of President Kennedy and his administration during the Cuban missile crisis.[388] Later, theorists of LMX concluded that leaders have an inner circle of trusted advisers which creates layers of trust through group roles that group dynamics extend to the boundaries of the group, thus excluding others from membership.[389] These studies have attempted to explain why people are willing to go to war or engage in conflict either from a biological or organizational standpoint. One assumes that animals are part of humanity's

---

[386] Lahti, David; Weinstein, Bret S. The better angels of our nature: group stability and the evolution of moral tension, Evolution and Human Behavior, Volume 26, Issue 1, 2005, Pages 47-63.

[387] Trivers, R. (2011). Deceit and Self-deception: Fooling Yourself the Better to Fool Others. United Kingdom: Allen Lane.

[388] Dansereau, Fred, Jr., George B. Graen, and William J. Haga. "A Vertical Dyad Linkage Approach to Leadership within Formal Organizations: A Longitudinal Investigation of the Role Making Process." Organizational Behavior and Human Performance 13 (1975): 46–78.

[389] Liden, R. C., Sparrowe, R. T., & Wayne, S. J. (1997). Leader-member exchange theory: The past and potential for the future. Research in personnel and human resources management, 15, 47-120.

past and the other focuses on recent current events to explain the social conditions that lead to war.

Jordan Peterson has attempted to explain our propensity for warfare as psychological malevolence born of evolutionary changes and genetic coding for the regulation of aggression in society through archetypes.[390] Psyche and soul are entomologically linked, "The soul who sins shall die. The son shall not suffer for the iniquity of the father, nor the father suffers for the iniquity of the son. The righteousness of the righteous shall be upon himself, and the wickedness of the wicked shall be upon himself" (Ezekiel 18:20). He would agree with Steven Pinker that human beings are improving our ability to work peacefully together. Yet, our experience in the 20th century has been one of great progress with unprecedented death and destruction. This is in keeping with the biblical admonishment, "You will hear of wars and rumors of wars but see to it that you are not alarmed. Such things must happen, but the end is still to come" (Matthew 24:6). While humanity improved technology, war increased. Christians uniquely act as redemptive agents in the world knowing that we still must deal with evil in our hearts, minds, and states.

The God of War

The Bible is a unified whole that explains the state of man and how best to achieve our ultimate purpose which is to glorify God. Christianity is an extension of Judaism and completion of the original covenant between God and man made to Abraham. Jesus said, "Do not think that I have come to abolish the Law or the Prophets; I have not come to abolish them but to fulfill

---

[390] Peterson, J. B. (1999). Maps of Meaning: The Architecture of Belief. United Kingdom: Routledge.

them" (Matthew 5:17). As scholar and author, N.T. Wright, (b. 1948) described, Christianity modified rabbinical practices and teachings, specifically on the resurrection, but these religious "mutations" occur within a strictly Jewish context.[391] God is consistently loving and just throughout the Bible. At the same time, God utterly, and repeatedly destroys people as recorded in the Old Testament for their wickedness and sin. God is immutable meaning that he is unchangeable in his existence, character, faithfulness, and wise plans.[392] Therefore, the triune God has the same being and purpose in the present as he did in the past.

The earth was flooded by water, either locally or globally, to wipe out unrighteous men and women. Noah and his family are preserved from this deluge. Sodom and Gomorrah were consumed by fire from heaven at God's command. Abraham begged Him appealing to his good judgment, "Will you indeed sweep away the righteous with the wicked? Suppose there are fifty righteous within the city. Will you then sweep away the place and not spare it for the fifty righteous who are in it? Far be it from you to do such a thing, to put the righteous to death with the wicked, so that the righteous fare as the wicked! Far be that from you! Shall not the Judge of all the earth do what is just?" (Genesis 18:25). God allowed Abraham to save his nephew Lot. Upon the destruction of the Egyptian army Moses sang that "The Lord is a man of war; the Lord is his name" (Exodus 15:3). After the Israelites are freed from Egypt because God sent severe plagues and death, they complete the conquest of the promised land under God's orders.

---

[391] Wright, N. T. (2003). The resurrection of the Son of God (Vol. 3). Fortress Press.
[392] Packer, J. I. (2021). Knowing God. United Kingdom: InterVarsity Press.

Undertaking this war was enacted as a judgment against the wickedness of the Canaanites at the orders of God (Deuteronomy 7:1-2; 20:16-18). He promised Abraham, "In the fourth generation your descendants will come back here, for the sin of the Amorites has not yet reached its full measure" (Genesis 15:16). God not only endorses this type of war but commanded a form of total warfare. The destruction of Canaanite tribes included the death of every man, woman, and child which must have been difficult for soldiers to see through. But Joshua carried out God's command. But, the Hebrews failed this order, taking plunder from pagan tribes, intermarriage and relationships continued against his decree. Any modern objection to this command must consider that our morality has been shaped by our Judeo-Christian heritage which prohibits humans from committing murder and genocide. The conquest of the promised land was God's just judgment on a wicked people by killing them to remove them from the territory which would become the kingdom of Israel, not ethnic cleansing.

The Bible inculcates the values that are used to attack Christianity. Therefore, God demonstrates care for the poor, oppressed, orphaned, and alien, and demands just laws and just rulers. "As I live, says the Lord God, I have no pleasure in the death of the wicked, but that the wicked turn from his way and live" (Ezekiel 33:11). God's judgment is not capricious. Many Old Testament scholars doubt the historicity of the events in Deuteronomy, viewing them as exaggeration or legends in support of the justice of their conquest. However, most Christians accept the veracity of the account. Divine command theory states that God is the source and measure of morality, and thus has no moral duties imposed on himself.[393] We do have obligations and prohibitions given to us by God. But God has the right to take life and can order the Canaanites, guilty of child sacrifice and pagan rituals, to be killed. If children were killed, then he will judge their eternal souls and we may rest in his goodness.

Therefore, God is justified in his command vanquishing the Canaanites. By his command, the Israelites did not commit murder any more than a soldier or jail warden does in the course of their duties. God's destruction of Sodom and Gomorrah are precursors to this conquest. Before the birth of Jacob and Joseph and the enslavement of Israelites in Egypt, Abraham was told by God that their enslavement was necessary, "Know for certain that your offspring will be sojourners in a land that is not theirs and will be servants there, and they will be afflicted for four hundred years" (Genesis 15:13). God was patient with the Canaanites allowing them to become completely debased before launching this war against them.

We can assume that if they had turned from their evil ways, he would have spared them as he did with Nineveh but God in his omniscient knowledge knew that they would not.[394] We later see, "I knew that You are a gracious and compassionate God, slow to anger, abounding in loving devotion—One who relents from sending disaster" (Jonah 4:2b). He grew the nation of Israel during slavery and prepared them in the wilderness then ordering them to remove the Canaanite kingdoms "that they may not teach you to do according to all their abominable

---

[393] Alston, W. P. (2002). What Euthyphro Should Have Said. Philosophy of Religion: A Reader and Guide, 283-298.
[394] Hasker, W., Dekker, E., Basinger, D. (2000). Middle Knowledge: Theory and Applications. Austria: Peter Lang.

practices that they have done for their gods, and so you sin against the Lord your God" (Deuteronomy 20:18). God was able to foresee the future problems that would occur if the Israelite nation intermarried and adopted pagan practices (see: 1 Kings 11:2). God takes His holiness, separation, and consecration to a deadly and serious level. His judgments are swift and final, as C. S. Lewis (1898-1963) puts it, "Aslan is not a tame lion." The slaughter of the Canaanites was not a regular order for all time, as compared to Islamic jihad,[395] but unique to the time and place of Ancient Israel.

Modern Spiritual Warfare

C.S. Lewis wrote during World War II, "Christianity is a fighting religion."[396] While affirming God's creative work, he continues, "A great many things have gone wrong with the world that God made, and that God insists, and insists very loudly, on our putting them right again." G.K. Chesterton (1874-1936) wrote, "The true soldier fights not because he hates what is in front of him, but because he loves what is behind him."[397] Spiritual warfare is often manifested in our physical lives, "From the days of John the Baptist until now the kingdom of heaven has suffered violence, and the violent take it by force" (Matthew 11:12). While this world may be governed by the aggressive use of force, warfare is the last resort for Christians. J. C. Ryle (1816-1900) wrote, "Necessity is laid upon us. We must fight. There are no promises in the Lord Jesus Christ's epistles to the seven churches, except to those who 'overcome.' Where there

---

[395] Khan, M. A. (2009). Islamic Jihad: A Legacy of Forced Conversion, Imperialism, and Slavery. United States: iUniverse.
[396] Lewis, C. S. (2009). Mere Christianity. United States: HarperCollins.
[397] Chesterton, G. K. Illustrated London News, Jan. 14, 1911.

is grace, there will be conflict. The believer is a soldier. There is no holiness without warfare. Saved souls will always be found to have fought a fight."[398] War comes first in our hearts and minds before bullets are fired and blood is shed. And bloodshed may be prevented if the Holy Spirit transforms more individuals into the likeness of Christ through our witness.

Offensive wars of conquest are generally forbidden. Defensive wars of protection are encouraged. Preemptive war should be avoided but may be necessary. Exploration is needed and conflicts that ensue because of a clash of civilizations are unfortunate but expected. This type of conflict is surveyed in *The Columbus Initiative*. Religious beliefs remain a source of conflict, tension, and strife, but they are not the primary driver of warfare as many claimed. Human beings must live according to certain assumptions about the way the world works and thus how war should be conducted.[399] Dealing with aggression in a just war has been and will be necessary for Christians to preserve life and freedom. Humans cannot exist in a constant state of critique, questioning everything all the time.[400] We must act following our beliefs and values when encroached upon, as Constantine did when emperor. Further, it is our presuppositions about why we live, love, work, and play that give life meaning, because we are meaning-seeking and making people.

Our understanding of war allows Christian leaders to make correct judgments about the causes of war and draw lines around acceptable and unacceptable behavior. Just as governors punish

---

[398] Ryle, J. C. (1877). Holiness. United States: Cornerstone.

[399] Marsden, L. (2013). For God's Sake: The Christian Right and US Foreign Policy. United Kingdom: Zed Books.

[400] White, C. M. (2017). The Morality of National Defense: An Aristotelian-Thomist Account (Doctoral dissertation, University of Colorado at Boulder).

crimes, nations must prohibit violence on an international scale through a robust national defense. God gave us reason and conscience to guide us toward him and participate in the redemption of creation through the removal of sin. While our sin nature pollutes our character, it does not determine our choices. A leaders' will to do right plays a significant part in national decisions, "for as he thinketh in his heart, so is he" (Proverbs 23:7a). At this level, seeking justice is one reason why the character of leaders matters. Leaders can make commitments, change their minds, or have their minds changed with new information. Leaders must, "keep your heart with all vigilance, for from it flow the springs of life" (Proverbs 4:23). God's plan was accomplished by Constantine, a sinful man seeking to do right, to provide cover for and support the growth of the church. This view of history is concordant with the pattern of events that builds towards the achievement of God's redemptive plan.

15

The Christian State

WHILE CHRISTIANITY ORIGINATED in Jerusalem it rose to predominate Europe after the fall of the Roman Empire.[401] A constant series of internal battles took place as political leadership transitioned from the capital of Rome to Constantinople under the Byzantine Empire while the papacy asserted greater religious power over the Holy Roman Empire in central Europe. Then, European Christian culture faced an existential threat in the rise of Islam. In no small miracle, Christian kings and church leaders prevailed in this conflict of civilizations. Many of Paul's First-century letters, which make up about 28 percent of the New Testament text, were directed to Greek or Roman churches.[402] As of 2020, Christianity remains the largest religion in Europe by demographic statistics based on survey data.[403] But this may not continue if current trends hold over the coming decades. The orthodoxy of claimants' faith has waned. However, the relationship between Christianity and Europe is one of the most profound movements of ideas in ancient history, ushering in the modern scientific world.

Today, bipolarity exists in Europe in terms of religious affiliation and practice. Many people say that they are Christian by birth but few live out a life of faith. This is especially true of the

---

[401] "The Global Religious Landscape" Pewforum.org.
[402] Morris, L. (1990). New testament theology. Harper Collins.
[403] "Discrimination in the European Union", Special Eurobarometer, 493, European Union: European Commission, 2019, retrieved 8 November 2019

younger members, those aged twenty through twenty-nine in the millennial generation. The only nations that report at least 10 percent weekly church attendance in this demographic are Poland, Portugal, and Ireland.[404] Yet 76.2 percent of Europeans self-report as Christian.[405] Of this group of over 565 million people, 48 percent are Catholic, 32 percent are Orthodox, and 19 percent are Protestant. This reflects the historical influence of Christianity, not its present power. In democratic nations, Christianity is often at odds with government policy on abortion, marriage, and family matters. Simply consider the lack of religious strength and vapid falsity in the Christian Democratic Union of Germany.[406] In AD 301, Armenia became the first officially Christian nation in Europe.[407] In AD 380, the Roman Empire became Christian. Christianity has influenced philosophy, art, and science in Europe and around the world as the center of teaching moved to the United States during the Nineteenth and Twentieth centuries.[408] This chapter details the origins of the relationship between the Church and state that began after the fall of Rome and persisted through the Middle Ages. During this era, Europe under the influence of the Catholic church in Rome became known as the seat of Christendom.

This chapter will describe the history of the church in Europe during the early Middle Ages which remains controversial. For

[404] Bullivant, S. (2018). Europe's young adults and religion: Findings from the European Social Survey (2014-16) to inform the 2018 Synod of Bishops.
[405] https://www.pewforum.org/2011/12/19/global-christianity-regions/#europe
[406] Langenbacher, E. (2019). Twilight of the Merkel Era: Power and Politics in Germany After the 2017 Bundestag Election. United States: Berghahn Books.
[407] Panossian, R. (2002). The past as nation: Three dimensions of Armenian identity. Geopolitics, 7(2), 121-146.
[408] Koch, Carl (1994). The Catholic Church: Journey, Wisdom, and Mission. Early Middle Ages: St. Mary's Press. ISBN 978-0-88489-298-4.

example, Judith Herrin (b. 1942), an archeologist, attempts to tell the history of Christianity during the Middle Ages from the perspective of a non-believer.[409] This belies the fact that she was raised in a Christian culture, and is undoubtedly influenced by it. She can add detail and nuance to this story, yet as an atheist, she attempts to redefine facts or determine narratives about a religion she rejects. Would she or her colleagues presume to tell Muslims or Hindus what they think, believe, or should do? Let Christians speak for themselves. Likewise, during the Middle Ages, the rise of Islam is used to provide historical context to the Crusades which will be addressed in *The Columbus Initiative*. A section on the Spanish Reconquista uses various battles and leaders to mark the efforts to alter the playing field from a defensive strategy along the coastline to an offensive attack on Muslim strongholds. The Great Schism provides a comparative example of the political divisions in the Christian church. Eventually war shifts to conquest in the Middle East and the seat of Islam.

Christendom

Millennials are not only apathetic toward religious practice but openly reject theism, 91 percent in the Czech Republic have no religion and never attend services.[410] In Estonia, Sweden, and the Netherlands, 70 to 80 percent have no religious affiliation or practice.[411] In 1910, of all Christians in the world lived in

[409] Herrin, J. (2021). The Formation of Christendom. United States: Princeton University Press.
[410] Hamplová, D., & Nešpor, Z. R. (2009). Invisible religion in a "non-believing" country: The case of the Czech Republic. Social Compass, 56(4), 581-597.
[411] Bullivant, S. (2018). Europe's young adults and religion: Findings from the European Social Survey (2014-16) to inform the 2018 Synod of Bishops.

Europe.[412] By 2010, less than ¼ of the world's Christians were European, not because of an overall decline in religiosity or faithfulness but a marked secularization of Europe.[413] Christianity has grown rapidly elsewhere, spreading in Asia, Africa, and South America.[414] In the last century, Christianity has grown over 400 percent from 500 million people to well over 2.2 billion.[415] It remains the world's largest religion by affiliation only rivaled by Islam with about 1.6 billion people.[416] Of these groups, both Christian and Islam, only a portion practice faithfully at least in terms of regular attendance to religious ceremonies and adherence to certain laws, morals, and ethical standards.

As previously discussed, human beings are religious by nature, and we tend to organize the nation around an animating spiritual purpose. It is helpful to see that "the world is mainly split into three religious groups, those who associate with and practice a religion, those who associate with a religion but do not practice it, and those who have no religion at all."[417] We would categorize these groups in a general model as fundamentalist

---

[412] Skirbekk, V., Stonawski, M., & Goujon, A. (2011). Global Christianity: A report on the size and distribution of the world's Christian population.

[413] Voas, D., & Doebler, S. (2011). Secularization in Europe: Religious change between and within birth cohorts. Religion and Society in Central and Eastern Europe, 4(1), 39-62.

[414] Kim, S., & Kim, K. (2016). Christianity as a world religion: An introduction. Bloomsbury Publishing.

[415] Bellofatto, G. A., & Johnson, T. M. (2013). Key findings of Christianity in its global context, 1970–2020. International Bulletin of Missionary Research, 37(3), 157-164.

[416] Hasan, R. (2019). Exploring the Link between Islamic Doctrines and Development. Telos, 2019(188), 55-78.

[417] Kalezic, Ilijana, "We Have Just Enough Religion to Make us Hate, but not Enough to Make us Love one Another." (2015). Law School Student Scholarship. 667.

(15%), nominal (70%), and unaffiliated (15%).[418] Both Islam and Christianity have strong ethnic and geographic ties to culture. For example, it is stereotypical for a person born in Saudi Arabia to be Muslim and someone of Italian descent to be Catholic. However, where Islam grows with strict rules, enforcement, and pressure, Christianity relies on loose conformity and socialization which is fraying at the edges. Jesus rejected religious fanaticism. "Woe to you, teachers of the law and Pharisees, you hypocrites! You shut the kingdom of heaven in men's faces. You yourselves do not enter, nor will you let those enter who are trying to. "Woe to you, teachers of the law and Pharisees, you hypocrites!" (Matthew 23:13). Politics is primarily concerned with the acquisition and use of power; it is thus at odds with the Christian faith which at its origin shunned the legalism of Pharisaical religion in favor of personal relationships.

The term "Christendom" refers to Christian states in the Middle Ages and this earthly dominion is the focus of this chapter. This period encompasses 400 to 1400 when the church rose to power until the fracturing of central control which is to be addressed in the next book. *The Columbus Initiative* will address the Renaissance (1400-1600) as the climax of Catholic art and culture, the Age of Discovery (1419-1643), as the power of the church spread outside of Europe, and the Reformation (1517-1642) as the beginning of decentralization and fragmentation of church authority. Even though European Christianity remained a global force through the early 1900s, the idea of Christendom or a unified and universal church occupying a physical kingdom if not a geographically bounded nation-state faded after the Middle

---

[418] Pew Forum on Religion & Public Life (18 December 2012). "The Global Religious Landscape."

Ages. While the influence of the church remains a powerful force in world history, it became more appropriately distributed and widely reorganized.[419] If there is a Christendom today, it includes most of Western Culture. However, the changes that have occurred in Europe and America alone mitigate against the influence of a singular interpretation of scripture or hierarchy of power and administration.

The term "Christendom" originated with Alcuin (735-804), an English scholar from York who became a deacon in the Catholic Church and teacher in the court of Charlemagne.[420] He wrote that "Although the whole of Europe was once denuded with fire and sword by Goths and Huns, now, by God's mercy, Europe is as bright with churches as is the sky with stars."[421] These churches were outposts of spiritual growth in European kingdoms during the Carolingian dynasty following victories by Charlemagne.[422] From the Eleventh to Thirteenth centuries, Roman Catholicism rose to dominate the Christian church. The Crusades (1095-1291) were the most direct and concerted effort to extend the power of the European Christian church into the Middle East, retaking the Holy Land from Islamic rule.[423] The Caliphates, Islamic empires, began to spread from Arabia under Mohammad (570-632), Rashidun (632-661), and Umayyad

---

[419] Brouwer, S., Gifford, P., & Rose, S. D. (2013). Exporting the American gospel: global Christian fundamentalism. Routledge.
[420] Stofferahn, S. (2009). Staying the royal sword: Alcuin and the conversion dilemma in early medieval Europe. Historian, 71(3), 461-480.
[421] Sarah Morice-Brubaker. https://christianhistoryinstitute.org/magazine/article/charlemagne-idea-of-christendom
[422] Wallach, L. (1959). Alcuin and Charlemagne: studies in Carolingian history and literature (p. 198). Ithaca, NY: Cornell University Press.
[423] Asbridge, T. (2012). The Crusades: The War for the Holy Land. United Kingdom: Simon & Schuster UK.

(661-750).[424] Christendom was eventually split, in 1054, between Rome, representing the center of the Western Latin or Catholic branch of the church, and Constantinople, eventually representing the Eastern Greek Orthodox denomination.[425]

Constantine consolidated his ruling authority, the right to command, in Rome where the pope had led the European church for nearly three hundred years.[426] He also delegated power, the influence of his position and person, to Constantinople. This brought the church into the mainstream of Latin life while honoring the evangelistic mission of the church. In 330, the Roman Empire remained the most powerful army on the planet. Of the thirty-two popes between Peter (called the first) and Sylvester (285-335) under Constantine, each served an average of 7.77 years, and many were martyred. In 380, Emperor Theodosius I (347-395), issued the edict *De fide Catolica* proclaiming the Roman Catholic Church as orthodox and condemning all heresy. This would never have occurred if Constantine did not make Christianity legal and legitimate. All this served to strengthen the church against the Lombard tribes in Germany according to Paul the Deacon (c. 720-799).[427] During the papacy of Steven II (714-757), the lands of Northern Italy were claimed for the church with the military support of Pepin the Short (714-768). The Roman Catholic Church took an

[424] Morton, N. (2020). The crusades to the eastern Mediterranean, 1095-1291. In Christian-Muslim Relations. A Bibliographical History Volume 15 Thematic Essays (600-1600) (pp. 281-306). Brill.

[425] Posnov, M. E. (2004). The History of the Christian Church Until the Great Schism of 1054. United States: AuthorHouse.

[426] Norwich, J. J. (2011). The Popes: A History. United Kingdom: Chatto & Windus.

[427] Edel, A. (1907). History of the Langobards. United States: Department of History, University of Pennsylvania.

active role in shaping Western Culture by altering the laws and reducing the persecution of Christians.

This harkens back to the "Donation of Constantine" allegedly a legal transfer of authority from Constantine to the Catholic church under Pope Sylvester (285-335) as he neared his death in 337.[428] The Roman Empire, while crumbling, became completely Christian in 380, but remained a military dictatorship decending under Constantine's sons Constantine II, Constantius II, and Constans I through 476.[429] The authenticity of the documents, a letter, and contract, were disputed by Lorenzo Valla (1407-1457) in 1440 and are now considered forged and rejected by most historians.[430] An original document could only be authenticated to 850 which was likely a copy of an earlier version made around 755 by a scribe named Christophorus under Pope Steven II.[431] However, the forgery was a falsehood offered by the Roman Catholic Church meant to legitimize what had already been in force by the emperors, kings, and church.

Constantine most likely never intended his secular power to be transferred to the Pope thus endorsing church leadership as ruler over the empire. This is just one of many repeated examples of sinful overreach with political and moral compromise in the church. Christianity had to survive the actions of prideful and ambitious men that damaged the faith and witness of many genuine believers. According to the legend, Pope

---

[428] Angelov, D. (2009). The Donation of Constantine and the church in Late Byzantium. Church and society in Late Byzantium, 91-157.
[429] Barnes, T. D. (2013). Constantine: Dynasty, Religion and Power in the Later Roman Empire. Germany: Wiley.
[430] Zinkeisen, F. (1894). The Donation of Constantine as applied by the Roman Church. The English Historical Review, 9(36), 625-632.
[431] Franklin, C. V. (2013). History and Rhetoric in the Liber Pontificalis of the Twelfth Century. The Journal of Medieval Latin, 23, 1-33.

Sylvester I (314–335) cured the emperor of leprosy. He later met with Constantine and received exclusive rights over all church property throughout the empire. This gift supposedly established a separate kingdom of spiritual and temporal power in the major cities of church power in Rome, Antioch, Alexandria, Constantinople, and Jerusalem. Constantine purportedly recognized Rome as the home of the Holy See, the universal government of the Roman Catholic Church.[432] And ostensibly, he recognized land for the Pope in what would become the Vatican City built on the tomb of Peter (the head of the church) honoring Paul (the chief missionary and teacher) who were both martyred in Rome.[433]

Fresco of the Donation of Constantine, Thirteenth Century;
Santi Quattro Coronati, Rome

---

[432] https://www.state.gov/u-s-relations-with-the-holy-see.
[433] https://www.nationalgeographic.com/science/2006/12/news-st-paul-tomb-found-rome/

Under a pagan government, the rule of the king was law. Even in the Hebrew kingdom, the Jewish people traded the law of God for the rule of men. However, once a man is elevated to the position of a king, as demonstrated, his desire for power tends to have him grasping at the straws of divinity. A religious instinct tends to expand when in authority and become narcissistic. Therefore, this ongoing issue will remain, to whom will leadership be given and from whom is it taken? What is the process of selecting our leaders? How is elevating someone to a position of power justified? And, what are the standards of law? In the Judeo-Christian tradition, the Ten Commandments are the moral foundation of civil law. "So the law is holy, and the commandment is holy and righteous and good" (Romans 7:12). Rather than a king's voice and hand, natural law is founded upon a transcendent moral order expressed by God and written by men.

If this is the basis of law, how are these laws to be enforced? We must have moral men leading our state. Topics of hierarchy, power, authority, responsibility, accountability, loyalty, and justice are intertwined in the church and state. As Peter wrote, "Submit yourselves for the Lord's sake to every human authority: whether to the emperor, as the supreme authority, or to governors, who are sent by him to punish those who do wrong and to commend those who do right" (1 Peter 2:13-14). Kings that rule justly serve the lord, and those who do not violate his law. Western Europe essentially created two centers of power, competing for legitimacy. According to the emanate Founding Father John Adams, the US is said to be "a nation of laws, not of men"[434] but this is only partially true. We are a nation of political will. Our will is needed to enforce laws that conform to our

---

[434] Ferling, J. (1996). John Adams: a life. Macmillan.

religious standards. Over time this has resulted in many internal squabbles, coups, and wars. However, as Margaret Thatcher once said of economic concerns, there is no better alternative way to structure society.[435]

This institutionalization of power used Peter's position as the leader of the church in Jerusalem to establish a succession of earthly priests in Rome. Expanding the kingdom of heaven rather than gaining earthly power is the mission of the church. Yet, how should the church govern itself? What is the ecclesiastical structure of the church? To whom are we accountable on earth? What justice must be done in the name of the Lord? How should church discipline occur? These questions are never answered directly or completely in the Bible. In many cases, a series of verses, such as those on elders and deacons, must be cobbled together and properly interpreted to form the traditions of the church. Leaders and members have struggled to reconcile these debates throughout its history. The universal Church does not need or have buildings. "For as the body is one, and hath many members, and all the members of that one body, being many, are one body: so also is Christ. For by one Spirit are we all baptized into one body, whether we be Jews or Gentiles, whether we be bond or free; and have been all made to drink into one Spirit. For the body is not one member, but many" (1 Corinthians 12:12–14). The Church is a group of people who worship Jesus as Lord.

In a modern example, there is no guidebook on the non-profit or tax-exempt status of church property. And the claim that a church without property can meet in the homes

---

[435] Berlinski, C. (2011). There Is No Alternative: Why Margaret Thatcher Matters. Basic Books.

of Christians perpetually is naïve. Instead, we are the temple of God, "Or do you not know that your body is a temple of the Holy Spirit within you, whom you have from God? You are not your own, for you were bought with a price. So glorify God in your body (1 Corinthians 6:19-20)." But we still gather in buildings. Certainly, the purpose of the Church is not to establish boundaries or build playgrounds, theater seating, and parking lots. But, it does seem that to meet together a substitute for an earthly temple for the local church is required.

Likewise, Christians must deal with organizational leadership as a key factor in the success and failure of the church. Church leadership mirrors biblical history as God used flawed men to carry out His plans such as Moses and David. The Roman Catholic tradition references Matthew 16:13–19 to claim that there is a biblically mandated title of Pope as the father of the church. Jesus asked, "But who do you say that I am?" Simon Peter replied, "You are the Christ, the Son of the living God." And Jesus answered him, "Blessed are you, Simon Bar-Jonah! For flesh and blood has not revealed this to you, but my Father who is in heaven. And I tell you, you are Peter, and on this rock I will build my church, and the gates of hell shall not prevail against it. I will give you the keys of the kingdom of heaven, and whatever you bind on earth shall be bound in heaven, and whatever you loose on earth shall be loosed in heaven." This is first and foremost a declaration of Jesus' intention to establish his kingdom in the Church. Later "Jesus came to them and said, 'All authority in heaven and on earth has been given to me. Therefore, go and make disciples of all nations, baptizing them in the name of the Father and of the Son and the Holy Spirit, and teaching them to obey everything I have commanded you. And surely, I am with you always, to the very end of the age'"

(Matthew 28:18-20). He was preparing his disciples to lead this religious movement through teaching and miracles.

Roman Catholic tradition places Peter, one of the first disciples to be called by Jesus Christ as the leader of the early church in Rome. He is viewed as the first among the apostles. Elders who were pastors and priests established a form of succession based on Peter, even though none was ordered or even contemplated in scripture. Peter proved to be a natural leader, outgoing and charismatic yet his passion and commitment to Christ led to rash decisions.[436] He met Christ walking on the waters of the Sea of Galilee but succumbed to his doubts. Later, Jesus accused him of having "little faith" and told Peter that he would deny him three times. He wounded a soldier sent to arrest Jesus. After his resurrection, Jesus restored Peter three times on the shore of the same sea. And, he became the leader of the nascent church in Jerusalem. In contrast to the Roman Catholic views, Orthodox tradition states that the foundation of the church was the apostolic faith. Protestants claim that Peter's affirmation of the deity of Christ is the rock upon which the church is built. Regardless, the claim of headship in the Roman Catholic church in Europe during the Middle Ages was tied back to Peter.

---

[436] Harrington, Daniel J. "Peter the Rock." America, 18–25 August 2008. Accessed 9 October 2009: p. 30.

16

The Dark Ages

RATHER THAN DARK and gloomy, the early Middle Ages
are the adolescence of the Christian church in Europe. These
years are an important transition between the early church and
a more mature iteration of the faith. Chris Wickham (b. 1950),
a historian, in his book *The Inheritance of Rome* contends
that European identity was formed between 400 and 1000 in
the crucible of tribal conflict, preserved by scholarship and
an overarching ethic, while never fully embracing the role of
the Christian church in this process.[437] He underestimates the
importance of Christian and monastic scholars in the promo-
tion of education and social reforms. And he does not accurately
represent the threat posed by the Islamic Caliphates which were
poised to take over Europe. And yet, the identity formation
Wickman rightly alludes to is better understood as a merger of
Christian morality with Greek and Roman polity and military
strategies. This partnership saved many people from material
want and spiritual corruption in a continent rife with pagan and
tribal conflict while protecting the same landmass from many
attempted assaults and incisions from without.

By preserving the written truths of Christianity, the monks
and priests of the Middle Ages served the world.[438] This included

---

[437] Wickham, C. (2009). The Inheritance of Rome: Illuminating the Dark
Ages 400-1000. United States: Penguin Publishing Group.
[438] Riches, John (2000). The Bible: A Very Short Introduction. Oxford: Oxford
University Press.

the preserving influence of Irish Christians.[439] The Bible was a central driver of social changes. In the early Third Century, Origen of Alexandria included Philemon, Hebrews, James, 2 Peter, 2 and 3 John, Jude, and Revelation in the compiled text of the Bible.[440] At the First Council of Nicaea, in 325, under Constantine, the books of the Bible as established were discussed as canon however not codified.[441] In 331, fifty copies of this Bible were commissioned and issued under the Bishop Eusebius of Caesarea in Constantinople.[442] Athanasius, Bishop of Alexandria, on Easter of 367, issued a list of the New Testament as it is now in the Catholic Bible calling this "canonized" (*kanon-izomena*)[443] version the official one. The compilation and preservation of the Bible are some of the "small miracles" we often take for granted.[444] No other book of this historical size and magnitude has lasted intact for as long as the Bible.[445] From this point forward the text of the Bible as we have it was reproduced and distributed in the church.

[439] Cahill, T. (2010). How the Irish Saved Civilization. United States: Knopf Doubleday Publishing Group.
[440] Olson, Roger E. (1999), The Story of Christian Theology: Twenty Centuries of Tradition & Reform, Downers Grove, Illinois: InterVarsity Press, ISBN 978-0-8308-1505-0
[441] https://www.etsjets.org/files/documents/Chicago_Statement.pdf
[442] Lindberg, Carter (2006). A Brief History of Christianity. Blackwell Publishing. p. 15. ISBN 1-4051-1078-3.
[443] By the early 3rd century Origen of Alexandria included Philemon, Hebrews, James, 2 Peter, 2 and 3 John, Jude, and Revelation.
[444] Strobel, L., & Wells, J. (2017). International Council On Biblical Inerrancy. Evangelical America: An Encyclopedia of Contemporary American Religious Culture, 225.
[445] Lim, Timothy H. (2005). The Dead Sea Scrolls: A Very Short Introduction. Oxford: Oxford University Press.

Christian kingdoms in Europe were a bulwark against the Huns, Turk, Samarkand, Viking, and Muslim invasions.[446] While the goal of the church was to evangelize the nations of the world, it did not live up to this high calling in a complete sense. Often survival and warfare predominated the intentions of European kings. But even imperfect efforts of human beings guided by God have both temporal and eternal value. Western culture, like humankind, remains sinful, unrepentant, adversarial, and wicked. Yet, the purifying qualities of the Christian church are like salt on meat to preserve the world. The church is antagonistic toward wickedness and deception, "For we wrestle not against flesh and blood, but against principalities, against powers, against the rulers of the darkness of this world, against spiritual wickedness in high places" (Ephesians 6:12). In many cases, the base tendencies of secular leaders were tempered and mitigated by accountability to church leadership. Since Constantine, there were countervailing forces of church and state, and all men are corrupted by pride, avarice, and ambition. These independent centers of power are in tension. When kings and priests were at odds, they were forced to resolve differences and disputes amicably if possible or via war when necessary.

What differentiates earthly domination from just authority is submission to the highest authority. Critics of the church intentionally conflate the biblical admonition against sinfulness and unbelief with a legalistic attack on sinful lifestyles which criminalizes non-Christians as infidels. Often, these acts were meant to dissuade hypocrisy within the body of Christ. The doctrine of original sin is operationalized in evangelism

---

[446] Sinor, Denis (1990). "The Hun Period". In Sinor, Denis (ed.). The Cambridge history of early Inner Asia (1. publ. ed.). Cambridge [u.a.]: Cambridge Univ. Press. pp. 177–203.

to invite people into a saving relationship with Jesus and deal with doubts. This assumes the fallibility of human beings who often give in to temptation. While persecution of unbelievers occurred, this critique labels Christians as ardently intolerant as today's radical Muslims. Yet Christianity requires voluntary conversion, not subjugation. By uniquely opposing Christianity, modern atheistic secularists who call the influence of the church on public policy "theocratic" conflate civil laws developed over time with state-sponsored religion. Islam and national governments which are animated by ideological motives have been and now are more repressive than Western governments. This aspect of modern religion and public policy in Muslim countries will be discussed further. However, historically, Christianity has benefited the people of states in which it exercises moral influence.[447] Whatever damage has been wrought by Europeans and Christians, these groups overlap but are not the same, the good accomplished through Western Civilization must be placed in the balance. As we will see, much of the benefits we enjoy in the United States have roots in Christendom.

In comparison, politics and Islam were unified from its inception. Mohammed specifically set about on a mission, crusade, or in Arabic, *jihad* (holy war) to defeat polytheists and bond the Arabic culture with an expansive monotheistic religion. As Islam rose during the mid-seventh century in the Middle East, Christianity was on its back foot. In many ways the expansion of the church in its home region stalled during the Middle Ages. This could be viewed as a strategic advancement to a new home in Europe as the gospel spread to gentiles who were more open to the message of Christ. Retrenchment

---

[447] Latourette, K. S. (1937). A History of the Expansion of Christianity.

in the Middle East shows how mounting opposition reached a natural limit on the appeal of Christianity. Later, cross-contamination between European secular forces and religious ambition may have reduced the witness of Christians. But the earth-shattering truths of this faith needed to be digested over hundreds of years to be resolved. Many of the theological debates that took place in the Middle Ages were able to shore up the boundaries of orthodox interpretations in the face of various philosophical challenges.

The Rise of Islam

By 650, evangelistic missions were proving more effective in Europe than Asia and Africa. The apostle Thomas, who demanded proof of Christ's divinity and resurrection, like his fellow Apostles, gave his life in service to the gospel. He traveled to India, died a martyr, and his tomb is a monument to his willing sacrifice to this day. Yet, his mission represented the eastern limits of Christian attempts at expansion. Contact between European Christians and Asian animistic, shamanic, and totemic religions was highly limited.[448] The more isolated warring states of China and the Indian Gupta Empire were barely influenced by Christians between AD 400 and 1200.

Religious and cultural interactions are often facilitated by trade. In 494, a band of medieval Jewish merchants known as Radhanites began to facilitate most trade between the Christian and Asian peoples. They made it as far east as the Tang dynasty in China. In 720, their multiple trade routes were stalked by Muslim bands, and the system of trade was sublimated or demolished.

---

[448] Yang, Fenggang; Lang, Graeme (2012). Social Scientific Studies of Religion in China. Brill.

The Arabian Peninsula, the Red Sea, and the Persian Gulf served to link Eurasia to Africa with trade from East Africa, Europe, the Middle East, India, and even China.[449] But, these economic connections were always facilitated by non-Christian traders therefore the interaction between the east and west continents and their respective religions was limited. The Byzantine Empire based in Constantinople retained some contact with the Eastern Asian empires. Around 500, Cosmas Indicopleustes (d. 550), a traveler and author of *Christian Topography*, journeyed to Eritrea, Ethiopia, India, and Sri Lanka.[450] In 552, the Byzantine emperor, Justinian I, had smugglers dressed as Persians run silkworms from China to Constantinople.

Early forays into Africa by Christian missionaries mostly remained north of the nearly impassable Sahara Desert between the advent of Jesus and the Middle Ages. Christianity by extending the history of Jewish contact with Egypt where Joseph and Mary secretly hid Jesus for the first few years of his life, attempted expansion in Africa. After Jesus' resurrection, Philip, the apostle, encountered a eunuch along the trade routes between Judea and Egypt, "Now an angel of the Lord said to Philip, 'Rise and go toward the south to the road that goes down from Jerusalem to Gaza.' This is a desert place. And he rose and went. And there was an Ethiopian, a eunuch, a court official of Candace, queen of the Ethiopians, who was in charge of all her treasure. He had come to Jerusalem to worship" (Acts 8:26-40). According to church tradition, the Coptic Christian church in Egypt was later established by Mark the evangelist, around AD 42.

---

[449] Nicolle, David (2009). The Great Islamic Conquests AD 632-750. Osprey Publishing. ISBN 978-1-84603-273-8.
[450] The Christian Topography of Cosmas, an Egyptian Monk. (1897). United Kingdom: Hakluyt Society.

Christianity spread slowly in Africa under Roman persecution along the Mediterranean. In AD 300, King Ezana made Christianity Ethiopia's state religion. After the Council of Chalcedon (451) the Coptic Church split from the Greek Orthodox Church in Alexandria. Over the next 200 years, the Coptic Church gradually expanded due to the Christianization of the Aksumite Empire and Nubian kingdoms. But after AD 639, Egypt was taken over by its Islamic conquerors from Arabia who persecuted, taxed, or subsumed Christians and the church. Mohammad not only created a religion but a state-endorsed kingdom drawing power from its religious foundation. From the Arabian Peninsula, Mohammed's successors through the Rashidun and Umayyad Caliphates expanded the power, control, and influence of Arab culture and the Islamic religion.

At its high point a unified Caliphate spanned over 11 million square kilometers, "Under the last of the Umayyads, the Arabian empire extended two hundred days' journey from east to west."[451] Within this landmass, two forms of taxes were used by the Islamic Caliphate to control the population, the *kharja,* a percentage of production from farming and husbandry, and the *jizya,* a protection head tax on non-Muslims. This was coerced as a matter of religious law in the Qur'an, "Fight those who do not believe in Allah… nor follow the religion of truth, out of those who have been given the Book, until they pay the tax in acknowledgment of superiority, and they are in a state of subjection" (Surah 9:029). [452] The *zakat* tax paid by Muslims was used by the Caliphate for charity to the poor and infirmed.

---

[451] The History of the Decline and Fall of the Roman Empire (vol. I, 1776; vols. II, III, 1781; vols. IV, V, VI, 1788–1789). all London: Strahan & Cadell.
[452] M. H. Shakir. Tahrike tarsile Qur'an. New York City, 1983. https://quod.lib.umich.edu/k/koran/browse.html

During the Seventh Century, Central Europe, while in turmoil, was principally protected from Islamic attacks by the Roman Empire's traditional dominance of the Mediterranean Sea. The Byzantine Empire, still loyal to the Roman Church, now controlled the eastern edge of Asia Minor (modern Turkey) through the Bosporus Strait, leading into the Black Sea at Constantinople. In addition, Acre, Alexandria, and Carthage remained under Latin influence and Roman military control. Justinian I (482-565), Byzantine emperor from 527 to 565, attempted a *renovatio Imperii,* "restoration of the Empire."[453] He began recapitulating the Western Roman Empire through a conquest in the Vandal Kingdom in North Africa led by General Belisarius and the Ostrogothic kingdom through Italy led by General Narses. He exerted continued power over the Mediterranean and, in the west, attacked and defeated the Sasanian (Persian) Empire. Justinian later had Roman law rewritten under Catholic guidance as to the *Corpus Juris Civilis.*

Under Justinian's rule, Byzantine culture flourished, architecture advanced as he constructed twenty-five basilicas and the Hagia Sophia in Constantinople. He was called "the emperor who never sleeps" because of his tireless work, purposeful energy, and relentless commitment. His wife, Theodora, was orphaned at a young age and became an actress where she was likely prostituted. She then became Christian and abandoned the stage, becoming a seamstress. Justinian changed the laws so that he could marry her as a commoner, and she became his co-regent and trusted adviser. Justinian debated Christian doctrines and issued a ban on three publications that were deemed heretical known as The

---

[453] J. F. Haldon, Byzantium in the seventh century (Cambridge, 2003), 17–19.

Three Chapters, which included certain writings or letters of Theodore of Mopsuestia, Theodoret of Cyrus, and Ibas of Edessa. He later wrote that "there are two great gifts which God, in His love for man, has granted from on high: the priesthood and the imperial dignity." His view of his reign as divinely ordained shaped his actions as he continued, "The first serves divine things, while the latter directs and administers human affairs; both, however, proceed from the same origin and adorn the life of mankind" and when working in concert, "general harmony will result."[454] The emperor later unsuccessfully attempted to reconcile the heretical teachings of Monophysite Nestorianism (that Christ had distinct human and divine persons) in Syria and Egypt with orthodoxy affirmed at the Council of Chalcedon (451) which stated that Jesus had two natures in one person, essentially he was truly God and truly man.

Justinian I was considered the last Latin emperor and the high point of the Byzantine Empire. In the years following Justinian I, the Byzantine army was spread thin in attempts to defend a wide area. They were defeated by the Rashidun Caliphate at the Battle of Fahl on January 23, 635. Then Palestine, Jordan, and Southern Syria were occupied except for two cities: Jerusalem and the port city Caesarea. These battles, initiated by the Islamic empire, restarted cycles of violence in the Middle East stretching back to ethnic divisions between Jews and Arabs in the Abrahamic era. According to the Qur'an, "retaliation is prescribed for you in the matter of the slain... there is life for you in retaliation, O men of understanding, that you may guard yourselves" (Surah 2:178-9). After the death of Mohammed, the leadership of the Caliphate had shifted to a series of kings. The Rashidun,

---

[454] https://patrologiagraeca.org/patrologia/

which means "Rightly Guided", was led by Abu Bakr (573-634). Later Umar ibn Khattab (584-644) with his general, Khalid ibn al-Walid (592-642), took control of the Caliphate and captured the Jewish capital during the Siege of Jerusalem in April 637. Between 688 and 691, Abd al-Malik had the Dome of the Rock built on the Temple Mount, modeling mosaics and architecture after Byzantine structures such as the Church of the Holy Sepulcher.[455] David ben Abraham al-Fasi wrote that Muslims allowed Jews in Jerusalem to pray at the Temple Mount which was prohibited under Byzantine rule.[456]

After repeated failed campaigns in Syria, the command of the northern armies of the Rashidun caliphate was assumed by Grand Commander Abu Ubaidah. Al-Walid was demoted but served as a general. In separate campaigns, they captured much of Northern Syria by AD 636 consolidating control of the Levant by AD 640. Caesarea fell in 640 at the decisive Battle of Yarmouk, ending the Byzantine foothold in the region. By 639, the early Muslim Rashidun Caliphate took over much of Egypt and severed trade with India and eastern Asia. In 652, the Islamic navy facilitated a blockade of Alexandria. That same year Muslim maritime forces attacked the island of Cyprus.[457] Yemeni sailors were skilled navigators with Iranian and Iraqi shipwrights who traveled to Alexandria to enhance the Caliphate navy, later based in Acre, Tyre, and Beirut. Muslims boarded and defeated the Roman fleet in 655, during the "Battle of the

[455] Creswell, K.A.C. (1924). The Origin of the Plan of the Dome of the Rock (2 Volumes). London: British School of Archaeology in Jerusalem. OCLC 5862604.
[456] Al-Fasi, D. (1936). Solomon L. Skoss (ed.). The Hebrew-Arabic Dictionary of the Bible, 'Kitāb Jāmiʻ al-Alfāẓ.' New Haven: Yale University Press.
[457] Nicolle, David (2009). The Great Islamic Conquests AD 632-750. Osprey Publishing. ISBN 978-1-84603-273-8.

Masts" off Cape Chelidonia in Anatolia. Later, the Muslim fleet raided Anatolia and Greece. One of the last strongholds of the Byzantine Empire was conquered by Islamic forces in 640 and "the horrors committed in the city of Caesarea in Palestine" were shocking according to Coptic Bishop John of Nikiû.[458] Perpetual offensive warfare is commanded by the Qur'an "fight in the way of Allah with those who fight with you. And kill them wherever you find them and drive them out from whence they drove you out, and persecution is severer than slaughter (Surah 2:190-1)." In 639–640, Raqqa, a Christian city now in modern-day Iraq, was conquered by the Muslim army while fending off revolts in the surrounding areas.[459]

During the Rashidun Caliph under Uthman, Constantine III attempted to recapture the Levant but was defeated in Northern Syria. In 654–655, Uthman built up his navy and began a campaign to capture Constantinople, but it was cut short when he was assassinated. This blood feud continued as the Qur'an decreed, "Fight with them, whoever then acts aggressively against you, inflict injury on him according to the injury he has inflicted on you" (Surah 2:194-3). A civil war began with the murder of Uthman. Ali opposed Umayyad, in what is known as the First Fitna (656–661) and created the primary division in the religion. Uthman's cousin and governor of the al-Sham or Levant, Muawiyah Umayyad founded the Sunni branch. Shia Muslims believe that Ali is the rightful heir to Mohammed. Muawiyah won the war, banished Ali, and established the Umayyad Caliphate in

---

[458] International Conference on Galilee in Antiquity (2 : 1997 : Durham, N. C., MEYERS, E. (1999). Galilee Through the Centuries: Confluence of Cultures. United States: Eisenbrauns.

[459] Meinecke, M. (1996). Patterns of Stylistic Changes in Islamic Architecture: Local Traditions Versus Migrating Artists. United States: NYU Press.

661 as a dynastic, hereditary rule. Damascus became the capital. Christians and Greek-speaking Romans remained in charge of the administration of city functions under Islamic control. The Umayyad Caliphate expanded to reach the Iberian Peninsula (called Al-Andalus) and was eventually overthrown by the Abbasids in 750.

17

The Reconquista

THE RECONQUISTA WAS the name of the resistance and resurgence of the Christian kingdoms in the Iberian Peninsula fighting against Muslim armies. This "reconquest" began with the Battle of Covadonga in 718, and continued with the expansion of Christian kingdoms, ending with the fall of the Islamic Nasrid kingdom of Granada in 1492. Ardo, the last Visigothic king of Hispania, fought Muslim invaders in Septimania, present-day Catalonia, over many years, suffering losses until 720.[460] According to Margaret MacMillian, The Battles of Tours (732) rebuffed the Muslim seizure of France and bolstered positions in Spain. The Battle of Vienna (1532) became the bookend on the tumultuous Middle Ages where Europe faced challenges from Islam. What follows is a detailed, if high-level, account of the various battles fought in Spain during this timeframe. The purpose of this record is to provide evidence to support the claims a) Europe was under siege from an Islamic caliphate and fully justified in waging war for nearly 800 years to repel this invasion and b) this experience had a marked impact on notions of inherent and deep incompatibility between Christianity and other people groups and religions.

War was brought to the doorstep of Europe and the men who sacrificed their lives defending their families should be honored.

---

[460] Collins, Roger (1989). The Arab Conquest of Spain 710–797. Oxford, UK / Cambridge, US: Blackwell. p. 45. ISBN 978-0-631-19405-7.

The basis for warfare as determined by the state is not absolute and should conform to the Just War doctrines. The Columbus Initiative deals specifically with the Crusades which began during the Reconquista and the aspects of that conflict that were unjust. However, in the case of the Reconquista, mostly defensive wars, and the Crusades, mostly offensive sieges, the purpose was protective toward Europe. In 1212, Pope Innocent III declared the first crusade and supported the Christian Spanish armies with 70,000 troops at the Battle of Las Navas de Tolosa. It took nearly 800 years for Christian armies to fully "reconquer" European land that was occupied by Muslim invaders.

The Early Caliphate

A question that modern people may ask of this defensive effort is: what gives Europeans the right to exorcize those conquering armies of another religion when this was not afforded to indigenous people during the colonization of the New World? As a point of comparison, the Native Americans fought the European colonists, so we share the same right of self-defense. However, the first interactions between indigenous people and Europeans demonstrate that trade and not conquest was their priority. However, some militaristic conquests, especially by the early Spanish conquistadors, show the bloodlust and desire for dominance that did not comply with the Just War Theory. The dynamics around colonization and integration will be explored in greater depth. However, in the Middle Ages, European leaders believed that their people's existence was at stake. Islam, while providing certain architectural, scientific, and mathematical innovations, did not establish a modern civilization instead moving with violent speed and prowess. The power to repel a foreign invasion has always held the balance in military warfare, thus the importance of walls and forts. Islam ran into European fortifications, repelled at the Rome Tiber River in 848 by Pope Leo IV.[461] By overextending its influence Islamic Caliphate did not provide a system of self-rule under which individuals or kingdoms could thrive the way that the Church did. To achieve the necessary balance between church and state, the Crusades showed how each must cooperate with the other.

The conquest of Hispania by the Umayyad Caliphate began in 711 when the armies of Tariq ibn Ziyad ventured from West Africa into South-western Europe. His army of 7000 arrived with no option but victory after Ziyad burned the ships. It was accompanied by oppressive taxes, slaughter, rape, and torture not unlike some actions by Europeans during the takeover of the Americas. According to Ayaan Hirsi Ali (b. 1969), there are two versions of Islam based on the phases in Mohammed's life as recorded in the Qur'an. Mecca Muslims believe in acceptance and tolerance of the other Abrahamic faiths in Christianity and Judaism.[462] "There shall be no compulsion in religion; the right way has become distinct from the wrong way. Whoever renounces evil and believes in God has grasped the most trustworthy handle; which does not break. God is Hearing and Knowing" (Surah 2:256). And in another passage, "Had your Lord willed, everyone on earth would have believed. Will you compel people to become believers? No soul can believe except by God's leave, and He lays disgrace upon those who refuse to understand" (Surah 10:99). The early Sunni caliphate did not honor these words.

Muslims were run out of Mecca and fled to Medina where the religion grew. They sought to return to Mecca in *Umrah*,

---

[461] Kreutz, B. M. (2011). Before the Normans: Southern Italy in the Ninth and Tenth Centuries. University of Pennsylvania Press.
[462] Ali, A. H. (2017). The Challenge of Dawa. Hoover Institution Press.

a pilgrimage, for *Tawaf*, a religious marching ceremony, at the *Kaaba*, a holy building at this site. However, after the Qurayshi polytheistic Banu Bakr tribe broke the Treaty of Hudaybiyyah and attacked Mohammed, the Banu Khuza'a tribe allied with the Muslims and surrounded the city. Mohammed's writings and actions soon became more militant and violent. "When the Sacred Months have passed, kill the polytheists wherever you find them. And capture them, and besiege them, and lie in wait for them at every ambush. But if they repent, and perform the prayers, and pay the tax, then let them go their way. God is Most Forgiving, Most Merciful" (Surah 9:5). Medina Muslims believe in a worldwide jihad and exhibit intolerance and vehemence toward non-Muslims called unbelievers and infidels.[463]

King Roderic at the Battle of Guadalete 711,
by Bernardo Blanco y Pérez (1871)

---

[463] Ibid. Ali

In 711, Islamic Arab-Berber forces invaded Hispania. Tariq ibn Ziyad crossed the Strait of Gibraltar, victoriously engaging a Visigothic force led by King Roderic at the Battle of Guadalete. Later, cities and towns along the Spanish coast were raided or extorted by the Umayyad governor of North Africa Musa ibn-Nusayr who joined Tariq. The Al-Andalus emirate of Umayyad Caliph Al-Walid I was consolidated around his general Musa ibn-Nusayr by marrying him to Egilona, Roderic's widow. Al-Walid died soon after taking possession of the Hispanic lands. Ibn-Nusayr wanted to convert to Christianity and establish his kingdom in Spain. But he was killed by Al-Walid's successor Sulayman during a pilgrimage to Mecca in 716. Back in Spain, Pelagius of Asturias led a rebellion of Hispanic and Gothic tribes, including Astures, Galicians, Cantabria, and Basques, and defeated an army of the Umayyad caliphate led by emir Anbasa ibn Suhaym Al-Kalbi in the mountainous northern Hispania in Covadonga. This was one of the few European victories against the Umayyad invasion during the initial phase of conquest.

After over two decades of fighting, in 732, Christian military forces under the Frankish king Charles Martel finally beat back the army of Abdul Rahman Al Ghafiqi, Governor-General of al-Andalus. The Battle of Tours likely took place in camps and fields in between Tours and Poitiers in Francia. Some historians have entertained exaggerated claims that Al Ghafiqi had an army of 60,000 to 400,000 more than double that of Martel. However, Edward J. Schoenfeld[464] and Victor Davis Hanson[465]

---

[464] Schoenfeld, Edward J. (2001). "Battle of Poitiers". In Cowley, Robert; Parker, Geoffrey (eds.). The Reader's Companion to Military History. New York: Houghton Mifflin. p. 366.
[465] Hanson, V. D. (2001). America and the Western Way of War. Historically Speaking, 3(2), 6-7.

estimate that nearly equal forces of between 20,000 and 30,000 men met near the Clain and Vienne rivers near Tours. These Islamic armies and the people of Northern Africa were labeled by European Christians Moors (derived from the Roman term Mauretania, a referring to the area in present-day Morocco and Algeria) and during the Crusades called Saracens (a term that generally refers to militaristic, marauding, or plundering forces) found in *Doctrina Jacobi*, a commentary that discussed the Muslim conquest of the Levant.[466] Asturias was then founded as the Christian Kingdom in Hispania. In this area, the Christian *Chronica Prophetic* (883–884) was circulated which documents and emphasizes the incompatibility between Christian and Muslim people, religion, and culture, and demands the expulsion of Islam from Europe.[467]

---

[466] Ruelle, C. É. (1911). N. Bonwetsch. Doctrina Jacobi nuper baptizati. Journal des Savants, 9(7), 327-328.

[467] Wolf, K. B. (2008). Chronica prophetica.

Bataille de Poitiers, October 732, Palace of Versailles,
by Charles de Steuben (1837)

Origins of Jihad

During expansion of the Islamic dynasty, Muslims and
Christians were embroiled in constant warfare. Muslim jihad
ideology was ramped up in Al-Andalus by the Almoravids
and especially the Almohads. Ethnic tension rose within
the Islamic army between Berbers and Arabs who often saw
African Muslims as subservient. In 970, Umayyad and his vizier
Almanzor campaigned for thirty years conquering northern
Spain and sacking Santiago de Compostela Cathedral. Fiefdoms
known as *taifas* sprung up when Córdoba disintegrated in 1010.
Remaining Spanish Christians were harassed by Muslim raiders
and extorted with tributes (*parias*). The Córdoba emirate fell
in 1031. León, Navarre, and Catalonia united with aristocratic
kings and knights in fiefdoms for fighting wars against Islamic

cities with peasant armies. By the time of the Second Crusade, the three kingdoms were powerful enough to conquer Islamic territory held in Spain. Later, Castile, Aragon, and Portugal conquered Islamic territories in 1212, in the Battle of Las Navas de Tolosa. Pope Innocent III called upon the Christian forces of King Alfonso, Sancho VII, and Peter II to defeat the al-Nasir caliph.

Battle of Las Navas de Tolosa, by Francisco de Paula Van Halen (1864)

During the period of the Crusades, Pope Innocent III called upon landed gentry to fight against Islamic armies in the European continent and the Holy Land. In a few cases, the Spanish kings offered leniency to defeated Muslims to curry favor and prevent future cycles of violence. However, this did not create lasting peace. The Mozarabs, Christians living under the Muslim Caliphate, were ethnically similar to Moorish Africans, therefore, assumed to be hospitable to Islam if well treated by emirs. Yet, when the African rebel Umar ibn Hafsun (850-917) returned to Spain after his exile in Morocco to avoid prosecution for various crimes, including manslaughter, he found the Mozarabs desirous of his particular set of skills.[468] The Mozarabs were harassed, humiliated, taxed exorbitantly, and killed by the emir, Abd ar-Rahman, and his successors. They asked Umar to lead an insurrection, which he did valiantly.[469] Umar later apparently converted to Christianity because of his need to integrate with the Mozarab church. Ann Christys, in her book, *Christians in Al-Andalus,* agrees with many scholars who think this was merely opportunistic because he oscillated between Christian and Muslim allegiances.[470] This indicates that he was willing to join with whichever force demanded his compliance, but it also shows that he was willing to change. He may have been simply a mercenary warlord, but the result of his leadership was to dull the attack of the Caliphate in Spain and protect the Church.

In 1120, Pope Callixtus II issued a papal bull named *Sicut Judaeis* (As the Jews) to protect the Jewish Europeans from the slaughter they experienced in the aftermath of The First Crusade. Then in 1123, he encouraged support for the Reconquista as part of The Second Crusade at The First Lateran Council. In the battle of Navas de Tolosa (1212), then at Córdoba (1236) and Seville (1248), Christian forces defeated Muslim strongholds in the Iberian Peninsula. Muslim occupation of Al-Andalus ended

---

[468] Safran, J. M, (2000). The Second Umayyad Caliphate: The Articulation of Caliphal Legitimacy in Al-Andalus. United Kingdom: Center for Middle Eastern Studies of Harvard University.
[469] Ye'or, Bat; Kochan, Miriam and Littman, David (2002) Islam and Dhimmitude: Where Civilizations Collide Fairleigh Dickinson University Press, Madison, NJ, p. 63 ISBN 0-8386-3942-9
[470] Christys, A. (2002). Christians in Al-Andalus, 711-1000. United Kingdom: Curzon.

when the Emirate of Granada surrendered to Spanish forces in 1492. As the last al-Andalus stronghold in the Iberian Peninsula fell to the army of Ferdinand and Isabella 100,000 Muslims were killed, 200,000 fled and 200,000 remained under Christian rule.[471] Edicts issued between 1499 and 1526 required Muslims in Spain to convert to Christianity. In 1609, Those who did not, mostly Muslim and Jewish inhabitants, were expelled from the peninsula by decrees of King Philip III and prosecuted by the Spanish Inquisition.

Summary Execution under the Moorish Kings of Granada,
by Henri Regnault (1870)

---

[471] Kamen, Henry. "Spain 1469 – 1714 A Society of Conflict." Third edition. pp. 37–38

The Great Schism

The Coptic Christian faction in Egypt was the first geographic and theological division of the church. But the first significant internal conflict took place in 1054 during the split between the East and West branches of Christianity. Then, in 1517, the Protestant Reformation further rent the church and increased freedom of conscience. The Great Schism split Christendom based on capital centers, political empires, and theological differences. For a millennium the Christian world was measured by theological orthodoxy while attempting to keep the personal power and political ambition of kings and popes at bay. During this time, the Islamic world was less prone to theological differences but instead peppered by civil war, assassinations, and dynastic machinations. The Sunni/Shia split was perpetuated by the desire for the scepter of leadership not intellectual debates.

Using the strategically positioned city on the Bosphorus strait, Constantinople allowed royal and military envoys to quickly respond to outside assaults or dangers. Yet during the strategic move to decentralize power the seeds of division were planted. During the Middle Ages, the east flourished, while the west declined in power as it retrenched to preserve Christianity's intellectual and theological history. Splitting the church between the East and West was the result of the Constantinian strategy. By placing the seat of power spanning Asia Minor in present-day Turkey the balance shifted. The Great Schism divided the Roman Catholic Church and Greek Eastern Orthodox Churches. This falling out was based on ecclesiastical differences, how church leadership and power should be centralized or distributed, and theological disputes. The papal authority has been a recurring theme in church conflicts. But this began with practical differences rather than pure heresy. By 1050, the Pope's position as the Bishop of Rome and the claim of universal jurisdiction was at odds with the polity of the See of Constantinople, a leadership position, and the pentarchy, the church leadership council of the city.

Roman Catholic teaching on the procession of the Holy Spirit, known as filioque, was a debate about the economy of the Godhead in the trinity. Roman Catholic doctrine has the spirit proceeding from God the Father "and from the son" but the Eastern Orthodox Church claims that as a coequal person the spirit only proceeds from God. Also, there was a dispute on whether leavened or unleavened bread should be used in the Eucharist. Greek churches in Italy that did not conform to Roman practices on communion were closed in 1053. Then in retaliation, Michael I Cerularius (1000-1059), the patriarch of Constantinople, closed all Latin churches in the city. In 1054, Pope Leo IX sent a legation with Cardinal Humbert of Silva Candida to Constantinople to rebuke Cerularius. Hubert demanded Byzantine assistance in joining a war against the Normans in Francia. When Cerularius refused this request, Humbert excommunicated him from the Latin church on the spot. Humbert was then promptly kicked out of the city to return to Rome.

In 1182, a large-scale popular uprising after the ascent of Andronikos I Komnenos (1117-1185) to the throne resulted in the massacre of Roman Catholics in Constantinople. Latin Christians, especially Genoese and Pisan, who were often merchants and resented by the primarily Greek residents, were decimated. Nearly 4,000 people who were allowed to live were sold in the Turkish Sultanate of Rûm as slaves.[472] During the

---

[472] Nicol, Donald M. (1988). Byzantium and Venice: A Study in Diplomatic and Cultural Relations. Cambridge: Cambridge University Press. p. 107.

Crusades, Catholic armies responded by sacking Thessalonica in 1185, followed by Constantinople in 1204, and installing Alexios III. This allowed the crusaders to exert control over the major cities of Antioch, Constantinople, and Jerusalem.[473] Over time efforts to repair this separation have been made, however many Orthodox church leaders have been critical of ecumenical efforts to reunite the Eastern and Western churches.[474] Sadly, this is but one more example of the infighting that has become endemic of Christian traditions, but it speaks more broadly of the robust and hearty discussions that can take place in the church.

Was the Christian and European response to the Muslim invasion of Spain justified? Yes, the attacks on the western Mediterranean coast provoked defensive measures that became offensive in nature as the front exapnded into North Africa. Eventually this became the basis for the Crusades to the Holy Land in Israel and the Middle East which took place between 1095-1271. This series of wars rebuffed the Islamic caliphate to stall the advance of Islam and limit it to the Middle East. Following the Renaissance and during the Reformation, Christopher Columbus and many European explorers expanded the influence of Christendom to the New World and around the globe. This would not have been possible without the leadership of Constantine the Great in the early 4th century and the church that rose in the ashes of the Roman Empire.

---

[473] Nichols, Aidan (2010). Rome and the Eastern Churches: a study in schism. Ignatius Press.

[474] Marshall, D. (2016). Sin, Forgiveness, and Reconciliation: Christian and Muslim Perspectives : a Record of the Thirteenth Building Bridges Seminar Hosted by Georgetown University Washington, District of Columbia & Warrenton, Virginia April 27-30, 2014. United States: Georgetown University Press.

In the following book, *The Columbus Initiative*, we investigate the impact of Christian leadership during the Middle Ages, Crusades, and Age of Discovery. By considering the impact of a Biblical worldview on the movement of Europeans the Crusades and interactions with Native tribes must be put in context. Colonization cannot be understood absent the historical context and evangelical direction of European expansion. To appreciate the role of Christian African American and European American leaders in the eradication of slavery grasping the first 1000 years of Christendom is necessary. Throughout this journey we wrestle with resolutions to the contradictions between church and state. This will be followed by *The Lincoln Legacy*, which details the formation of America and its transition into a modern Republic under the Civil War, while exploring the nature of divisions and unity in the United States of America during the World Wars. Lastly, *The Reagan Compromise* is a capstone to address the modern dilemma of the Christian church dealing with secular forces in America and opposition abroad.

While the universal Church exists, it includes born-again believers throughout the world of many denominations who may disagree on inessential matters. There will not be a singular physical church gathering until Christ returns. Before Jesus' Second Coming, we meet in local churches as the "body of Christ" on earth. This openness that allows people to explore the truths of scripture while affirming orthodoxy is an important part of the Christian church. The challenge of allowing healthy debate but putting down false teaching and heresy remains to this day.